Into the Unknown:

The Logistics Preparation of the Lewis and Clark Expedition

Donald L. Carr, MAJ, USA

Combat Studies Institute Press,
Fort Leavenworth, Kansas

Foreword

Two hundred years ago, a 30-man US Army party—the "Corps of Discovery"—ascended the Missouri River and conducted the most extensive exploration yet attempted of the North American continent's interior. Their accomplishments in the two-year journey were remarkable, and bear testimony to the leadership acumen of Captains Meriwether Lewis and William Clark. The results were also a testament to the courage and fortitude of the soldiers they led. No successful operation, however, occurs in a vacuum. Detailed planning and preparation are often key elements in the eventual overall conclusion. In that vein, the preparations for the Lewis and Clark expedition were exhaustive. President Thomas Jefferson, father of the expedition, ensured Lewis was well prepared for his task by coaching, mentoring, and teaching the young officer for two years. Lewis and Clark then spent the better part of a third year planning and organizing for the journey. As a result, they had plans for almost every contingency imaginable. In addition, their mental preparation and agility enabled them to react to and take advantage of unforeseen circumstances.

Major Donald Carr's *Into the Unknown: The Logistics Preparation of the Lewis and Clark Expedition* is a valuable study examining the key logistics components and considerations in the planning and execution of the mission. Modern logisticians will find themes in transportation, civilian contracting, indigenous (host nation) support, and others that still resonate today. Major Carr clearly demonstrates that Captains Lewis and Clark, in facing the daunting tasks of the great expedition, rose to the challenges and met them with ingenuity, detailed planning, discipline, leadership, and resolution—hallmarks worthy of reflection by today's junior leaders.

Thomas T. Smith
Lieutenant Colonel, Infantry
Director of Combat Studies

Preface

Captain Meriwether Lewis' task was to equip and man a party to traverse the unmapped middle third of the United States. Most studies of the expedition begin with the party's departure from Camp Dubois in the spring of 1804. This starting point ignores the important logistics planning, preparation, and training that commenced with Lewis' appointment as personal secretary to President Thomas Jefferson in the spring of 1801. Under President Jefferson's watchful eye, Lewis conducted extensive preparations at Washington, DC; Harper's Ferry, Virginia; Philadelphia; Pittsburgh; and St. Louis.

Expedition journals, personal correspondence, and equipment receipts are used to provide insight into the effectiveness of the endeavor's logistics support plan. The study concludes by identifying four themes evident in the expedition's planning and execution that are useful to modern logisticians: the value of innovation, the significance of support received from indigenous peoples, the employment of civilian contractors, and the seemingly obligatory discovery that transportation capabilities rarely meet requirements.

Contents

Illustrations

Chapter 1

Introduction

Nearly all examinations of Meriwether Lewis and William Clark's expedition begin with presupposition that America's favorite explorers commenced their journey from St. Louis in the spring of 1804 (See Figure 1). In actuality, preparation for the expedition began more than a year earlier. Rarely do historians pause to consider the value of logistics preparation. Thus, logisticians have become accustomed to reading history devoid of the toils of their predecessors. This study is different. As both an Army logistician and a fledgling historian, I will review the expedition's foundation to identify issues and themes that might be useful to modern logisticians.

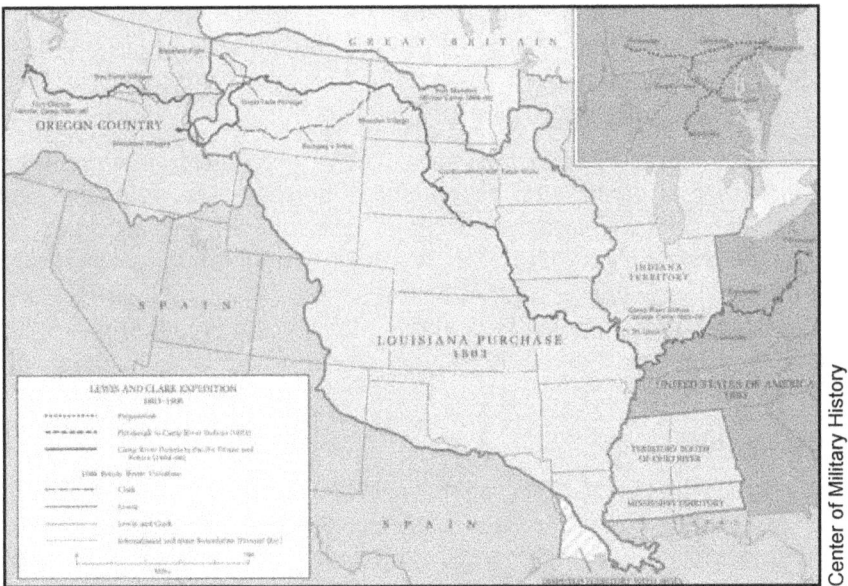

Figure 1. Lewis and Clark Expedition Trail

Lewis, as the expedition's primary logistics planner, collected supplies and equipment in Virginia (including the area that would become West Virginia) and Pennsylvania in 1803. After departing Pittsburgh, Lewis, with a small transitory crew, traveled down the Ohio River, meeting Clark and several men he recruited near Louisville. At the junction of the Ohio and the Mississippi Rivers, the growing crew turned north en route to St. Louis, where yet more men and equipment were acquired. Expedition members built Camp Dubois across the river from Spanish-controlled St. Louis to pass

1

the winter of 1803-1804. This critical phase of the expedition, preparations undertaken from Virginia to Camp Dubois, is the focus of this study.

The logistics questions confronting Meriwether Lewis and William Clark are essentially the same questions that confront today's logistics planners. The primary question to be answered is: How does a logistician prepare to venture into the unknown? Secondary questions include:

1. How was Lewis' logistics plan derived?
2. Was his plan adequate?
3. If his plan fell short, how did expedition members compensate?
4. What mix of men and equipment was required?
5. Was civilian contractor support anticipated?
6. To what extent was support from native peoples anticipated?
7. Why did Lewis choose his former commanding officer, William Clark, to accompany him?
8. How would medical care be provided?

The answers to these questions will be obtained from expedition journals and from correspondence between participants and supporters. The questions outlined above will be analyzed in light of four of 11 of the US Army's current logistics functions: transportation, supply, combat health support (medical support), and human resource support. By analyzing expedition preparations in this manner, it is hoped that new insights, useful to modern planners, will be discovered.

Background

By the close of the 17th century, Spain had firmly established footholds in the area that now comprises Texas, New Mexico, and Arizona. Within an additional 100 years, Spanish explorers, while engaged in a search for a water route from Spain through North America to India, extended their holdings and influence to include southern California.[1] Seafaring explorers from Spain, Britain, Russia, and America had developed limited trade relationships with native peoples and had mapped the Pacific coast, but had not journeyed significantly inland. Most important, the Pacific Northwest was not definitively claimed by European powers. As the 18th century came to a close, the majority of the North American continent remained uncharted by American and European explorers.

France and Spain, also seeking a water route connecting New Orleans with the Pacific Northwest, alternately controlled the huge center swath of territory west of the Mississippi and east of the Rocky Mountains. Both nations constructed a series of fortifications and fur trading outposts beside the Missouri River, stretching from St. Louis to the Mandan Villages, located in the vicinity of modern-day Bismarck, North Dakota.[2] Travel west of the Mississippi was limited to fur traders and other adventurers. Areas north and west of the Mandan Villages were uncharted territory. Figure 2 illustrates just how little was known about the continent's geography. Note that the western two-thirds of the modern United States is depicted as blank space.

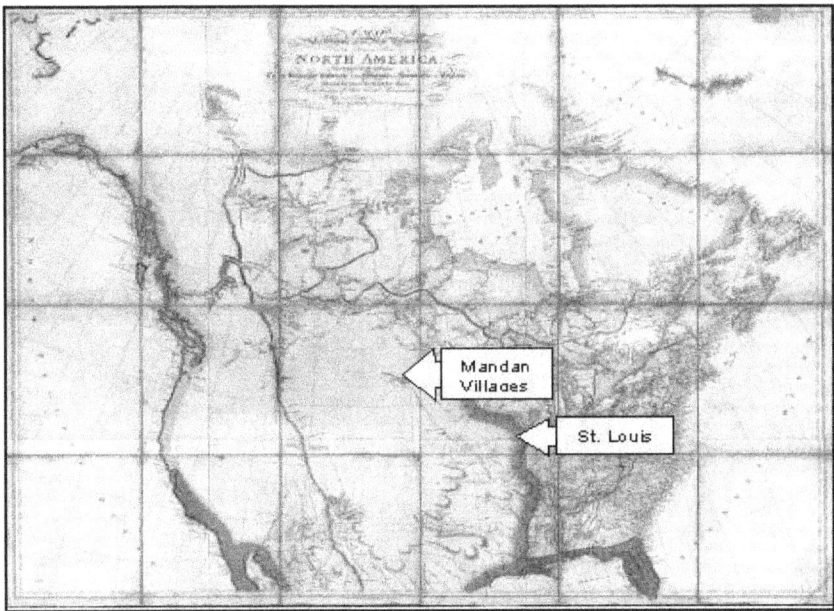

Figure 2. 1802 map by Aaron Arrowsmith,
with text boxes added.

Americans of the period thought of the lands west of the Appalachian Mountains as the untamed frontier. The overwhelming majority of citizens would never travel farther than 50 miles inland from the Atlantic. It is in this context that Lewis was solicited to design an expedition to discover a water route to the Pacific. He spent from January 1803 to May 1804, a full 16 months, formally pondering and planning the optimal mix of men, equipment, and provisions. This immense planning effort continued even while President Jefferson waited impatiently for the expedition's departure.[3]

Jefferson's Guidance

President Thomas Jefferson's vision was of an American nation stretching unbroken from the Atlantic to the Pacific.[4] He was of the opinion that the United States would be far better off if the citizens on the western banks of the Mississippi were American citizens rather than subjects of Britain, France, or Spain. He also recognized that if America could discover a water route from the east to the Pacific Ocean, the fabled Northwest Passage, trade and American domination of North America would be accelerated.

The expedition had its official genesis in the winter of 1803, when President Thomas Jefferson confidentially sought approval from Congress on 18 January 1803. Jefferson communicated his tentative plan:

> An intelligent officer with ten or twelve chosen men, fit for the enterprise and willing to undertake it, taken from our posts, where they may be spared without inconvenience, might explore the whole line, even to the western ocean, have conferences with the natives on the subject of commercial intercourse, get admission among them for our traders as others are admitted, agree on convenient deposits for interchange of articles, and return with the information acquired in the course of two summers.[5]

Jefferson sought approval from Congress for two reasons. First, as is the case today, he needed financial backing for the operation. Based on a figure provided by Lewis, the president sought $2,500. Second, he thought that the support of the Congress might discourage rival powers from obstructing the expedition's mission.[6] Although at this point the expedition was essentially a secret mission, President Jefferson communicated his intent to explore the lands west of the Mississippi to the governments of France, England, and Spain. His correspondence with foreign governments stressed his desire to further science and literature; privately he spoke of commerce and trade.[7]

Jefferson's short-term objective was trade with the dozens of Indian tribes known to inhabit the uncharted lands west of the Mississippi River. His secondary mission was the advancement of science. In addition to serving as president of the United States, Jefferson also served as president of the American Philosophical Society, headquartered in Philadelphia. The American Philosophical Society was the home of nearly all serious scientific thought for the fledgling nation. Much of Meriwether Lewis' logistics and scientific preparation was conducted in Philadelphia and assisted by Jefferson's philosophical society colleagues.

Jefferson had a lifelong interest in exploration and science. He was influenced by the accomplishments of British maritime explorers during the latter half of the 18th century. Jefferson undoubtedly developed his appreciation for science and exploration from a world dominated by James Cook. During the 1760s, Cook, a British naval officer, explored and surveyed the waters off Labrador, Nova Scotia, and Newfoundland. "His outstanding work on those surveys made Cook the prime candidate to lead what would be three epic voyages of discovery to the Pacific." His final voyage had the same objective as the Lewis and Clark expedition—to find the Northwest Passage.[8]

During the spring of 1801, Jefferson was captivated by a recently published account of Alexander Mackenzie. Mackenzie was a fur trader and explorer employed by the North West Company who, 10 years after the fact, published a volume titled *Voyages from Montreal, on the River St. Lawrence Through the Continent of North America, to the Frozen and Pacific Oceans in the Years 1789 and 1793*. It has been speculated that Mackenzie's book was among the fewer than a dozen books carried to the West Coast by Lewis and Clark.[9] While Mackenzie's book related a daring journey, it offered little to quench Jefferson's thirst for hard scientific data.

Jefferson, eager to counter the encroachment of European nations on the North American continent, while at the same time hoping to further science, made three unsuccessful attempts to send explorers westward. While a member of Congress in 1783, he attempted to recruit William Clark's older brother and Revolutionary War hero, George Rogers Clark, to lead an expedition. Citing poor health and other commitments, George Clark rejected the offer.[10] In 1792, Jefferson, while serving as secretary of state, sought to enlist physician and botanist Dr. Moses Marshall in a voyage up the Missouri River with the intent of discovering a route to the South Sea. Apparently Marshall also declined.[11] In 1793, on behalf of the American Philosophical Society, "Jefferson sponsored a more promising effort by André Michaux, a French botanist." Michaux's task was to "find the shortest and most convenient route of communication between the U.S. & the Pacific ocean, within the temperate latitudes, & to learn such particulars as can be obtained of the country through which it passes, it's productions, inhabitants & other interesting circumstances." Michaux's exploration attempt failed to penetrate the Mississippi River but succeeded in providing Jefferson with the "basic outline" for the Lewis and Clark expedition.[12]

It should be noted that a 19-year-old family acquaintance, Meriwether Lewis, also volunteered to command Jefferson's 1793 endeavor. It is likely that Jefferson was impressed with the nerve demonstrated by the young Lewis. It is widely acknowledged that after monitoring Lewis' Army career, Jefferson selected him to serve as his personal secretary to harness his passion for exploration demonstrated nearly a decade earlier. Thus, Lewis had the benefit of planning alongside the president from the summer of 1801 through the summer of 1803. Lewis and Clark planned and prepared collaboratively from August 1803 to May 1804. Rarely are logisticians afforded the luxury of focusing on a single plan for such a significant length of time, nor is it common to receive meticulous guidance directly from the president of the United States. But this was no ordinary mission.

Notes

1. Reuben Gold Thwaites, *Original Journals of the Lewis and Clark Expedition* (New York: DSI Digital Reproduction, 2001), 1:xviii–xix.

2. Ibid., 1:xxxii.

3. Ibid., 1:43–44.

4. Donald Jackson, ed. *Letters of the Lewis and Clark Expedition, with Related documents: 1783-1854*, 2 vols., 2nd ed. (Urbana: University of Illinois Press, 1978), 2:654.

5. Ibid., 1:12.

6. Ibid., 1:13.

7. Ibid., 1:10-13.

8. James P. Ronda, "'Knowledge of Distant Parts,' The Shaping of the Lewis and Clark Expedition," *Montana The Magazine of Western History* (Autumn 1991), 6.

9. Jackson, 1:56.

10. Moulton, Gary E., ed. *The Definitive Journals of Lewis and Clark*, 11 vols. (University of Nebraska Press, 2002-2003), 2:1.

11. Moulton, 2:2.

12. Ibid.

Chapter 2

Logistics Planning

Jefferson's Instructions

As already discussed, President Jefferson had been planning the exploration of the western half of the continent for his entire adult life. On 7 April 1805, upon departing his wintering site for his final push west, Lewis romantically described the expedition as a "da[r]ling project of mine for the last ten years" and likened his "six small canoes, and two large pirogues" to the fleets of Columbus and Cook.[1] By spring 1803 Lewis had been Jefferson's secretary for almost two years. The pair had probably spent many hours considering the mission's complexities. Together they crafted the instructions that would guide the mission's execution. While Jefferson's final guidance to Lewis was not published until late June 1803, there is little doubt Lewis understood the president's intent while he gathered supplies and equipment during the preceding months.

National Park Service

Figure 3. President Thomas Jefferson

The president sought suggestions from his cabinet regarding the expedition's instructions. Albert Gallatin, the Treasury secretary, in his response dated 13 April 1803, stressed the importance of carrying out a thorough geographic survey of the lands that were to be settled by the people of the United States. Gallatin also outlined a concept that foreshadowed nearly exactly the strategy selected when he suggested that Lewis:

7

ought to take, on the Spanish side of the Illinois settlement, some person who had navigated the Missouri as high as possible & it might not be amiss to try to winter with the traders from that quarter who go to the farthest tribe of Indians in the proper direction. A boat or canoe might be hired there (at the Illinois) to carry up to that spot a sufficient quantity of flour to enable him to winter there with comfort so that his band should be fresh & in good spirits in the spring.[2]

Jefferson also incorporated suggestions provided by Levi Lincoln, his attorney general. Lincoln was concerned with the political implications of the expedition's failure or destruction. If the endeavor failed, he predicted that Jefferson's political enemies might use the president's personal involvement in the project to inflict political damage. He suggested that Jefferson imbue the project with the goal of providing western religion to native peoples along the route.[3] Lincoln further argued that if the mission failed while attempting to "improve" Indian religion and morality, conservative New Englanders would have to temper their criticism.

Jefferson penned Lewis' formal instructions only two weeks prior to Lewis' departure from Washington, the majority of logistics preparation having already been concluded at Harper's Ferry, Virginia, Lancaster, Pennsylvania, and Philadelphia. His 55-foot keelboat, in which he would lug the expedition's equipment and rations to a wintering location west of the Spanish settlement of St. Louis, was (he thought) near completion in Pittsburgh. For sure, Lewis was not surprised by anything in Jefferson's final instructions.

Jefferson recognized the importance of the expedition's mission and the influence it would have on future generations. By providing detailed instructions he hoped to communicate his broad vision while ensuring that certain specific tasks were accomplished. A transcription of Jefferson's instructions is provided at Appendix A.

The military character of the expedition is prominently depicted in the document's salutation, "To Captain Meriwether Lewis esq. Capt. Of the 1st regimt. of Infantry of the U.S. of A." What follows is a military order from the commander in chief to a mission commander. The document's second paragraph outlines the logistics preparation that had largely already taken place.

Instruments for ascertaining, by celestial observations, the geography of the country through which you will pass, have been already provided. Light articles for barter and presents among the Indians, arms for your attendants, say for from 10. to 12. men, boats, tents, & other traveling apparatus, with ammunition, medicine, surgical instruments and provisions you will have prepared with such aids as the Secretary at War can yield in his department; & from him also you will receive authority to engage among our troops, by voluntary agreement, the number of attendants above mentioned, over whom you, as their commanding officer, are invested with all the powers the laws give in such a case.[4]

Jefferson also states that the nature of the mission has been "communicated" to the governments of France, Spain, and Great Britain. This declaration was probably intended to deflect the political impact of the expedition's potential interdiction by foreign agents.

The primary purpose of the expedition being the establishment of new trade routes, Jefferson specified that Lewis' mission was to "explore the Missouri river, & such principal stream of it, as, by it's course & communication with the waters of the Pacific Ocean, may offer the most direct & practicable water communication across this continent, for the purposes of commerce."[5] Since the prospect of future trade required the willing participation of native peoples, Lewis was instructed to "treat them in the most friendly & conciliatory manner which their own conduct will admit. . . ."[6] Jefferson further directed Lewis to identify merchandise desired by the Indians to assist future traders. In his most interesting pair of proposals Jefferson instructs Lewis to extend an offer to raise and educate Indian children and to offer influential chiefs an opportunity to visit Washington. The latter Lewis manages to achieve.

Jefferson's vision of the expedition was of a dozen or so men, much like the successful Mackenzie expedition across the Canadian Rockies discussed earlier. Not wanting the expedition to appear too extravagant, Jefferson specified a small defensive force made up of soldiers already on the government's payroll. His instructions stated that the expedition's 10 to 12 men would be "sufficient to secure you against the unauthorized opposition of individuals or of small parties: but if a superior force, authorized, or not authorized, by a nation, should be arrayed against your further passage, and inflexibly determined to arrest it, you must decline it's farther pursuit, and return." It would appear that Jefferson was concerned for the safety of the expedition participants. In actuality it is probable that Jefferson was interested in safeguarding the information contained in expedition journals more than the lives of the participants.[7] However, Jefferson did exhibit genuine concern for expedition participants and the natives they would encounter by directing Lewis to ensure that "some matter of the kinepox"[8] be carried to inoculate members against smallpox, an ailment that "for centuries had been a great killer of the white man."[9]

Jefferson desired to receive the expedition journals rapidly. He specified that once on the West Coast, Lewis was to locate a vessel of any nation and attempt to return two "trusty people" with a copy of the journals. He also authorized a return of the entire party by sea by way of "cape horn or the cape of good hope" if it was deemed too dangerous to return over land. To pay for passage, as well as to replace worn-out equipment and clothing, Jefferson offered an open letter of credit authorizing foreign governments and American agents around the globe to seek reimbursement for aid rendered to expedition members.[10]

The final portion of the instructions relates to succession of command. Clark is not mentioned in the document; however it can be assumed that Jefferson approved of his participation since Lewis' invitation to Clark was penned the previous day. Jefferson authorized Lewis to name his successor "by any instrument signed & written" in his hand from his party demonstrating "superior fitness."[11]

Lewis' Logistics Plan

Lewis' support plan was altered as the mission evolved. Much can be gleaned from the items Lewis sought prior to his departure, however. A list of supplies and equipment Lewis requested from facilities in Virginia and Pennsylvania is located at Appendix B. A listing of equipment and supplies received from facilities in Virginia and Pennsylvania is found at Appendices C and F. A listing of equipment and supplies acquired during Lewis and Clark's trip down the Ohio and at their wintering site of 1803-1804 is provided at Appendix H.

One must select a moment in time to begin the process of analysis. I have selected 19 June 1803 because, as discussed earlier in this chapter, Jefferson's instructions were only hours from completion and Lewis was in the process of drafting perhaps the most remarkable invitation in American history. By this date Lewis (see Figure 4) had already spent two years working closely with the president refining equipment lists. As his westward departure drew near, Lewis began to experience some apprehension about the depth of responsibility he was about to undertake.

He recognized that the mission required an additional officer, one whose skills and attributes would complement his own. Lewis' first choice was William Clark. We remain unsure as to whether Clark knew of a pending invitation. In his letter of acceptance, dated 18 July 1803, he declares, "the enterprise &c. Is Such as I have long anticipated."[12]

National Park Service

Figure 4. Meriwether Lewis

This statement leaves to the imagination the possible conversations that he and Lewis might have had while serving together on the frontier. One point is clear—Jefferson may have approved Lewis' request for a second officer, but he had little to do with selecting Clark (see Figure 5). Lewis' letter of invitation is charged with enthusiasm. In his dramatic style he outlines the mission's purpose and provides a status of his logistics preparations. This letter, when considered along with the various lists of supplies and equipment, provides a reliable means of ascertaining Lewis' interpretation of Jefferson's intent and his plan to achieve it. Lewis' letter to Clark is only half as long as Jefferson's instructions, but it manages to capture the essence of the operation as well as his concept for supporting the anticipated 18-month voyage. Only the concept for providing medical support was omitted. This omission was probably not an oversight. An expedition consisting of two officers and 10 to 12 men implied medical self-sufficiency. The lack of a physician would not be considered odd at the time when one Army physician attended approximately 450 men.[13]

Figure 5. William Clark

Lewis communicated that he had been managing logistics preparations in Lancaster and Philadelphia since early March and that preparations were almost complete. He named Pittsburgh as his point of embarkation and stated that he plans to depart Washington for Pittsburgh at the end
of June with the intent of arriving at Clark's location of Clarksville (named
for his brother George and located in Indiana) by 10 August 1803.[14]

Personnel

Lewis communicated to Clark his belief that Jefferson, with congressional approval, would grant Clark a permanent captain's commission.
Lewis then made an extraordinary offer to his longtime friend. He proposed to Clark that if he agreed to join the party that his "situation . . . in
this mission will in all respects be precisely such as my own."[15] In essence
he was offering his friend co-command of the expedition. The depth of
friendship between these two men is remarkable. Lewis' intense respect
and trust is illustrated by his invitation's closing remark, "if therefore there
is anything under those circumstances, in this enterprise, which would
induce you to participate with me in it's fatiegues, it's dangers and it's

honors, believe me there is no man on earth with whom I should feel equal pleasure in sharing them as with yourself."[16]

In his letter Lewis repeats the now-familiar expedition personnel authorization of "noncommissioned officers and privates not exceeding 12, who may be disposed voluntarily to enter into this service." He then goes on to add that he is "also authorized to engage any other men not soldiers that [he] may think useful in promoting the objects or success of this expedition."[17] In his instructions Jefferson authorizes payment to "consuls, agents, merchants, or citizens of any nation" that render aid to the expedition.[18] But Jefferson's statement is in the context of aid rendered in the form of sea transportation from the Pacific back to Washington. Thus, the basis of Lewis' impression that he had unlimited authorization to hire non-soldiers is not directly attributable to Jefferson's instructions.

During his trip down the Ohio, Lewis communicated to Clark that it was his intention to "engage some good hunters, stout, healthy, unmarried men, accustomed to the woods, and capable of bearing bodily fatigue in a pretty considerable degree."[19] Using his questionable authorization to hire civilian contractors, Lewis also planned to "engage some French traders at Illinois to attend me to my wintering ground with a sufficient quantity of flour, pork, &c. To serve them plentifully during the winter, and thus be enabled to set out in the Spring with a healthy and vigorous party."[20]

Lewis' personnel estimate, in addition to causing him to determine the need for another officer, required two distinct groups of enlisted men to facilitate the mission. The first group would be quickly assembled for the purpose of transiting the Ohio River. The second group, or permanent party, would be hand selected from the forts on the frontier and would accompany him to the Pacific. Civilians with skills deemed essential, such as guides and interpreters, would be hired as necessary in accordance with Lewis' interpretation of Jefferson's instructions.

Supply

Lewis noted to Clark that he had secured letters of credit to obtain supplies.[21] As noted earlier, the letter of credit was intended for use in emergencies and for securing sea transportation from trade vessels around the "summer or the beginning of Autumn" of 1804.[22] This estimate would prove overly optimistic since the party would be forced by political concerns and shortening days to spend the winter of 1803-1804 across the river from St. Louis, where Lewis planned to acquire a stock of "flour, pork, &c. to serve them plentifully during the winter," which would enable his party to set out the following spring "with a healthy and vigorous party."[23] During the long winter Lewis would teach Clark how to operate the scientific equipment acquired in Philadelphia.

Ironically, the scientific aspect of the expedition, featured prominently in Jefferson's instructions, is saved for Lewis' closing paragraphs where he states, "the other objects of this mission are scientific"[24] and that he intends to "collect the best possible information relative to whatever the country may afford as a tribute to general science."[25] He goes on to state that his "instruments for celestial observation are an excellent set and my supply of Indian presents is sufficiently ample."[26]

Lewis grouped his supplies into nine categories: Mathematical Instruments, Arms and Accoutrements, Ammunition, Clothing, Camp Equipage, Provisions and Means of Subsistence, Indian Presents, Means of Transportation, and Medicine. A complete list of the supplies requested and received at Harper's Ferry, Philadelphia, and Pittsburgh can be found in Appendices B, C, and F.

Transportation

Lewis' transportation plan appears simple enough. He would embark from Pittsburgh on a 55-foot keelboat, descending the Ohio River until it met the Mississippi. He would then turn north toward St. Louis and the mouth of the Missouri River. Next he would ascend the Missouri several thousand miles against the current. Once the keelboat became impractical, due to its size and draft, it would be discarded in favor of "canoes of bark or raw-hides." At the base of the Rockies, expedition members would portage necessary supplies and equipment "to the waters of the Columbia or Origan River and by descending it reach the Western Ocean." [27] It should be noted that based on secondhand information received from natives and traders during the winter of 1804-1805, Lewis and Clark believed that "there might yet be an easy passage to the Columbia."[28]

Lewis was aware that the mouth of the Columbia was situated approximately 140 miles south of Nootka Sound, a sizeable European trading post where he anticipated that it would be "easy to obtain a passage to the United States by way of the East-Indies in some of the trading vessels that visit . . . annually."[29] In the unlikely event that the expedition failed to make contact with European traders, Lewis planned to retrace the route that had led him to the West Coast.[30]

The only hints we have that Lewis expected to make use of horses are a single line on a shipping manifest detailing the movement of "Capt. M. Lewis' Goods"[31] from Philadelphia to Pittsburgh in the spring of 1803 and a single sentence in a letter from Jefferson to Lewis relating to the

14

shipment of a saddle from Washington to Pittsburgh in July 1803. The treasury was billed only one dollar for the transportation of the single box of "Horsemans Cloths." The fee to transport Lewis' horseman's clothes was less than any of the remaining 34 boxes in the same shipment. Lewis apparently viewed the operation as primarily a waterborne endeavor.

Medical

Jefferson and Lewis both appreciated the dangers expedition members would be exposed to. In the early 19th century, injury and disease often resulted in death at an early age. Hence, relatively insignificant wounds by today's standards would likely prove life threatening to Lewis and his men.

Arguably the best medical mind in the United States in 1803, Dr. Benjamin Rush, was recruited by Jefferson to provide training and advice. Lewis "would serve the shortest medical apprenticeship in American history—about two weeks."[32] Lewis received his medical training and assembled his medical kit while in Philadelphia during the last two weeks of May 1803.

Lewis would begin gathering his equipment soon after the president received congressional authorization to conduct the expedition in February 1803. His first stop would be the new arsenal at Harper's Ferry.

Notes

1. Gary E. Moulton, ed., *The Definitive Journals of Lewis and Clark*, 11 vols. (Lincoln: University of Nebraska Press, 2002-2003), 4:10.
2. Donald Jackson, ed., *Letters of the Lewis and Clark Expedition, with Related Documents: 1783-1854*, 2 vols., 2nd ed (Urbana: University of Illinois, 1978), 1:131.
3. Jackson, 35.
4. Ibid., 61.
5. Ibid.
6. Ibid., 64.
7. Ibid.
8. Ibid.
9. Eldon G. Chuinard, *Only One Man Died: The Medical Aspects of the Lewis & Clark Expedition* (Fairfield, WA: Ye Galleon Press, 1998), 102.
10. Jackson, 1:65.
11. Ibid.
12. Ibid., 110 –111.
13. Chuinard, 47.
14. Jackson, 1:57.

15. Ibid., 60.
16. Ibid.
17. Ibid., 58.
18. Ibid., 65.
19. Ibid., 58.
20. Ibid., 59.
21. Ibid., 57.
22. Ibid.
23. Ibid., 59.
24. Ibid.
25. Ibid.
26. Ibid., 60.
27. Ibid., 58.
28. Moulton, 5:1.
29. Jackson, 1:58.
30. Ibid., 59.
31. Ibid., 92.
32. David J. Peck, *Or Perish in the Attempt: Wilderness Medicine in the Lewis and Clark Expedition*, (Helena, MT: Farcountry press, 2002), 47.

Chapter 3

Harper's Ferry

On 14 March 1803, roughly two months before Jefferson completed his final instructions, Lewis departed Washington for the newly established Harper's Ferry Armory (See Figure 6). He was armed with a letter from Henry Dearborn, Jefferson's secretary of war, addressed to Joseph Perkins, the armory's superintendent. The short letter directed Perkins to "make such arms & Iron work, as requested by the Bearer Captain Meriwether Lewis and to have them completed with the least possible delay."[1] Located at the juncture of the Potomac and Shenandoah Rivers, approximately 40 miles northwest of Washington, the armory was a logical first destination for Lewis for two reasons. First, his estimate called for the fabrication of a collapsible iron boat frame that he expected would take armory craftsmen some time to construct. This collapsible boat, fondly referred to by historians as the *Experiment*, will be discussed later.[2] Second, he wanted to provide the resident arms makers with adequate time to complete their work on the 15 rifles he planned to supply to newly enlisted expedition participants. His request for 15 rifles is roughly in line with the 13 participants, "an intelligent officer with ten or twelve chosen men," called for in Jefferson's request for appropriation of 18 January 1803. It can be assumed that at this point Lewis planned the additional two rifles as spares or as weapons intended for civilian contractors engaged along his route.

Figure 6. Harper's Ferry Arsenal, circa 1803

"By 1801 the Harper's Ferry Armory was producing its first weapons. At that time the workmen were skilled artisans drawn from the Philadelphia area. Their specialty was individual piecework, but the armory was able to begin mass production of rifles shortly after Lewis' visit."[3]

Rifle Debate

For students of the Lewis and Clark Expedition, there is no more controversial topic than that of the type of rifle procured by Lewis at Harper's Ferry. It is generally assumed that Lewis procured 15 Harper's Ferry Model 1803 rifles, America's first regulation US Army rifle. After all, Harper's Ferry prepared 15 rifles for Lewis in the spring of 1803. It has been very neat for historians to accept the coincidence. Others believe that Lewis did not draw Model 1803 rifles, although he might have unwittingly helped to inspire them. The type of rifles acquired by Lewis was introduced and perfected in Pennsylvania but is more commonly identified as belonging to the family known as Kentucky Rifles (see Figure 7).

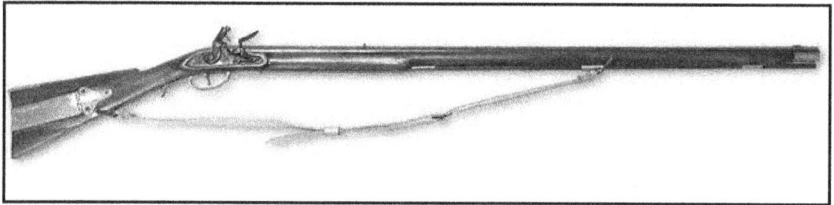

National Park Service

Figure 7. Pennsylvania (Kentucky) Rifle, c. 1803

On 20 April 1803, Lewis wrote to Jefferson from Lancaster, Pennsylvania to report that he had just completed four and a half weeks' work at Harper's Ferry seeing to the preparation of 15 rifles and to the construction of his iron canoe. Over a month later, on 25 May, Secretary of War Dearborn sent the following letter to Joseph Perkins:

> There being a deficiency of rifles in the public Arsenels, and those on hand not being as well calculated for actual service as could be wished. It is considered advisable to have a suitable number of judiciously constructed Rifles manufactured at the Armory under Your direction. You will therefore take the necessary measures for commencing the manufactory as Soon as may be after completing the Muskits now in hand. The Barrels of the Rifles should not exceed two feet nine inches in length and should be calculated for carrying a ball of one thirtieth of a pound weight.

Clearly this letter directed the development of what would become the Model 1803, while noting that the armory was currently engaged in producing the Harper's Ferry 1795 musket.[4] In his book *Harper's Ferry and the New Technology*, Merritt Roe Smith establishes that "a small quantity of full-stocked rifles may have been made at Harper's Ferry on an experimental basis in 1800 or 1801, but the War Department did not issue an official directive for the preparation of arms of that type until May 25, 1803."[5] Model 1803 rifles are half-stocked weapons. When using the term "experimental," Smith implies that the weapons on hand were there for routine repairs to test newly acquired armory equipment and to validate armory procedures rather than to create prototypes of a rifle that had not yet been directed. Smith goes on to point out that the armory submitted "several patterns" to the war department for approval in November 1803. He further argues that because of the rural culture that existed in the Harper's Ferry region in the early 19th-century change came slowly. In fact, Smith states that armory workers were "sadly deficient" in a "social milieu" adaptable to change and regimentation. Workers considered themselves artists and labored according to their own timelines, normally structured around maintaining their farms.[6] Most of the armory's less than two dozen gunsmiths had been trained in the Lancaster-Philadelphia area, where the Pennsylvania (Kentucky) rifle was born.[7] The gunsmiths probably owned and hunted with Pennsylvania rifles. The highly regarded *Flayderman's Guide to Antique American Firearms and their values* solicits readers to "note Kentucky rifle influence on most parts" of the Model 1803.[8] Harper's Ferry possessed a skilled but traditional work force. It is highly unlikely that, in one month's time, armory gunsmiths managed to hastily create a prototype Model 1803 in a facility that had yet to produce its own rifles (to Dearborn's specifications) before being directed to do so.

In his latest edition of his aptly named *Definitive Journals of Lewis and Clark*, Gary Moulton states in a footnote that Lewis received:

> at least fifteen of the new Model 1803 rifles, the first ones issued; this weapon, the first rifle specifically designed for the U.S. Army, was about .54 caliber with a thirty-three-inch barrel, but the expedition version may have been a predecessor or prototype differing in some respects from the standard issue. The captains sometimes referred to them as short rifles, because they were considerably shorter than the civilian Kentucky long rifles of the period.[9]

Stephen Ambrose, in his book *Undaunted Courage,* states that Lewis received "U.S. Model 1803, the first rifle specifically designed for the U.S. Army, .54-caliber, with a thirty-three-inch barrel."[10] In Carl Russell's much-quoted work *Guns of the Early Frontiers*, in referring to the Harper's Ferry Model 1803, states that "it is known also that in 1803 the Lewis and Clark party obtained a few pieces of this model."[11]

Ambrose and Russell are wrong on this point. The Lewis and Clark Expedition did not employ Harper's Ferry Model 1803 rifles. Russell manages to quote the actual correspondence from Secretary of War Dearborn that directs the model's initial development but omits the fact that the letter was penned after Lewis had already reported that "My Rifles, Tomahawks & knives are already in a state of forwardness that leaves me little doubt of their being in readiness in due time."[12]

Only Moulton, after stating that the expedition received Model 1803 rifles from Harper's Ferry, acknowledges the debate by adding that the weapons may have been prototypes of the 1803. An argument that has been used in favor of the use of Model 1803 rifles is the following journal entry written by Clark on 20 March 1806 as it appears in the 1893 Coues edition of the expedition's journals:

> Finding that the guns of both Drewyer and Sergeant Pryor were out of order, the first was *fitted with a new lock, and the broken tumbler of the latter was replaced by a duplicate, which had been made at Harper's Ferry, where the gun itself had been manufactured* [emphasis added]. But for our precaution in bringing extra locks, and duplicate parts of the locks, most of our guns would be now useless, in spite of the skill and ingenuity of John Shields in repairing them. Fortunately, as it is, we are able to record here that they are all in good order.[13]

In Moulton's edition of the journals, the same passage appears this way:

> The Guns of Sergt. Pryor & Drewyer were both out of order. the first had a *Cock screw broken which was replaced by a duplicate which had been prepared for the Locks at Harper's Ferry* [emphasis added]; the Second repared with a new Lock, the old one becoming unfit for use. but for the precaution taken in bringing on those extra locks, and parts of locks, in addition to the ingenuity of John Shields, most of our guns would at this moment been entirely unfit for use; but fortunate for us I have it in my power here to record that they are in good order, and Complete in every respect."[14]

Apparently Elliot Coues significantly edited Clark's notes, incorporating his bias in favor of Model 1803 rifles. *Flayderman's Guide* points out that the "Model 1803 is best known as an issue weapon for the Lewis & Clark Expedition" and then notes that the 1803 possesses "graceful lines and Kentucky rifle styling," which are important factors in the model's popularity with collectors.[15] As we will see, Lewis' rifles were Kentucky rifles modified in such a manner as to pose striking resemblance to future Model 1803 rifles.

Kirk Olson, the owner of a potentially authentic Lewis and Clark Pennsylvania rifle and author of *A Lewis and Clark Rifle?*, argues that the "15 rifles made for Lewis were not prototypes or patterns of the Model 1803 but were instead predecessors in the evolution of the 1803 rifle."[16] Olson states that in addition to the rifle he owns, he is also aware of an authenticated full-stock Harper's Ferry Pennsylvania-style rifle dated 1803 that has a brass patch, both almost identical to that of the Model 1803. He then asserts that both rifles were modified 1792 contract rifles (see Figure 8).

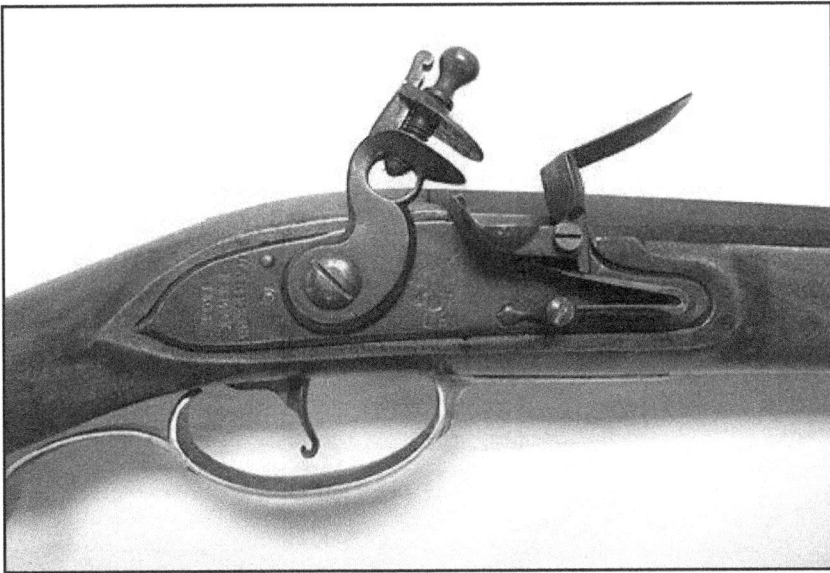

Figure 8. Reproduction 1792 Militia Rifle

National Park Service

In 1792 the United States had not yet begun to produce its own arms, and rifles were procured from private gun manufacturers. In the same year the president established a "battalion of riflemen, consisting of four companies, each company composed of eighty two privates. Arms for arming these riflemen were purchased from well known makers of the 'Kentucky Rifle' in Pennsylvania."[17] Olson drives his argument home by directing the reader to three photos and descriptions of 1792 contract rifles in the

Flayderman's Guide. Three different manufacturers produced the rifles, and all three are full-stocked, yet they each display remarkable similarities to the Model 1803.[18]

When Lewis went to Harper's Ferry looking for 15 rifles, he was not seeking to create a new rifle type, nor would it be logical to do so. Expedition members would rely on their weapons for sustenance as well as self-defense. Lewis required spare locks so that repairs could be made along his route without specialized tools. According to Olson, Lewis sought to avoid filling and drilling while in the field. The solution provided by Harper's Ferry gunsmiths was duplicate locks and an assortment of spare parts.

Hence, Lewis headed west with 15 1792 contract Pennsylvania rifles with shortened barrels to facilitate use in rough terrain and on watercraft. He had spare locks, capable of being swapped out without filling or drilling, that would prove to be reparable by a single skilled private, the expedition's gunsmith, John Shields.

Lewis' *Experiment*

Lewis intended to spend about one week at Harper's Ferry communicating his requirements and then proceeding to Lancaster for scientific training scheduled by Jefferson. On 20 April 1803, he wrote a letter to Jefferson to explain why he was behind schedule.

> My detention at Harper's Ferry was unavoidable for one month, a period much greater than could reasonably have been calculated on; my greatest difficulty was the frame of the canoe, which could not be completed without my personal attention to such portions of it as would enable the workmen to understand the design perfectly.[19]

Lewis was convinced of the utility of having a collapsible boat (see Figure 9) capable of being easily portaged around the "falls of the Missouri situated five hundred miles above Fort Mandan" and the Rocky Mountains.[20] Because of inaccurate information received from the Mandans and traders, Lewis and Clark grossly misjudged the enormity of the obstacles in their path. In a letter to his mother, penned at Fort Mandan, Lewis shared his belief that the portage from the Missouri's source to the south fork of the Columbia River is "a distance not exceeding half a days march."[21]

The iron boat was to see its first use after completing a grueling 18-mile, month-long portage over rough terrain around the Great Falls of

Figure 9. Reproduction of a section of the collapsible iron boat frame

Montana. While Clark searched for a suitable portage route, Lewis managed other preparations for the portage. He had men hunt elk with the intent of both stockpiling and drying meat, and for obtaining the more than two dozen hides necessary to cover his boat's frame. On 16 June Lewis assigned six soldiers the task of constructing primitive carts to haul supplies over the portage route.[22]

The portage route proved too difficult to allow the men to transport the expedition's heavier equipment on their backs. The captains decided to emplace their second cache of the journey near the base of the falls. Presumably to be recovered on the return trip, food, weapons, powder, and tools were buried (a listing of cached items, locations and recovery dates is located at Appendix I).[23] Ironically, the only discussion of employing horses during this period can be found in Lewis' journal entry dated 16 June. The entry contemplates the expedition's ability to acquire horses from the Shoshone Indians to cross the larger-than-anticipated, snow-tipped Bitterroot Mountains looming to the southwest. The party's "Indian woman" (Sacagawea) was ill. Lewis speculates that Sacagawea, being a Shoshone, is the expedition's "only dependence for a friendly negociation with the Snake Indians [Shoshone] on whom we depend for horses to assist us in our portage from the Missouri to the Columbia River."[24]

Lewis and Clark had now observed the series of five falls that make up Montana's Great Falls. They realized that the veracity of the information received during the winter of 1804-1805 caused them to significantly underestimate the

23

difficulty of the portage. They knew that they had also received their information regarding the Rockies from the same sources. Lewis had undoubtedly gained a greater appreciation for the necessity of Shoshone guides and horses to support the expedition's crossing of the Rocky Mountains. To meet the Shoshone they would first have to negotiate the Great Falls.

Lewis' iron boat, weighing approximately 100 pounds,[25] was hauled to the far side of the falls, most likely on the carts previously mentioned, and assembled between 18 June and 8 July 1805. Lewis was unable to find appropriate pine tar to seal the boat's seams formed where animal skins were sewn together. He also lamented the method selected to sew the skins together because tears developed as the skins dried. Prior to use, most of the skins were scraped clean of fur. After the boat was almost complete, Lewis realized that the lack of fur hampered the use of a substitute for pine tar made from charcoal, beeswax, and buffalo tallow.

When the craft was finally launched on 9 July 1803, according to Lewis, "she leaked in such a manner that she would not answer."[26] Upon conceding the boat's failure, he ordered that it be sunk to recover the skins used in its construction for other uses. After the skins were recovered, the iron frame was cached because as Lewis lamented, it " could probably be of no further service to us."[27]

The failure of the iron boat created an additional challenge. The captains now had to find a way to "convey the stores and baggage which we had purposed carrying in the boat."[28] Between 9 July and 14 July, a work party led by Clark constructed two additional canoes required to carry the equipment that was to be transported by the iron boat. On the morning of 15 July 1805, the expedition, with 33 personnel and baggage, continued its journey westward in eight canoes.

After squandering a month of prime traveling weather supervising the fabrication of the frame at Harper's Ferry in the summer of 1803 and then wasting an additional month attempting to get his experiment to float at the conclusion of an arduous portage around the Great Falls, Lewis was mortified at his boat's performance.

The captains would now scrutinize the assumptions made during their stay at Fort Mandan and Camp Dubois. The expedition did not anticipate the need for horses to facilitate their portage of the Great Falls. Had they done so it would have made possible an earlier, and significantly less treacherous, crossing of the Bitterroot Mountains. In this chapter we have discussed Lewis' preparations at Harper's Ferry; now it is time to turn our attention to the locale that facilitated Lewis' scientific and medical training and provided the bulk of the expedition's equipment, Pennsylvania.

Notes

1. Donald Jackson, ed., *Letters of the Lewis and Clark Expedition, with Related Documents: 1783-1854*, 2 vols., 2nd ed (Urbana: University of Illinois, 1978), 1:76.

2. Jackson, 1:39.

3. Joseph D. Jeffrey, "Meriwether Lewis at Harper's Ferry," *We Proceeded On*, vol. 20, no. 4 (November 1994): 16.

4. Norm Flayderman, *Flayderman's Guide to Antique American Firearms and their values* (DBI Books, 1994), 434.

5. Merritt R. Smith, *Harper's Ferry Armory and New Technology* (Ithaca, NY: Cornell University Press, 1977), 53.

6. Smith, 33-35.

7. Ibid., 57.

8. Flayderman, 440.

9. Gary E. Moulton, ed., *The Definitive Journals of Lewis and Clark*, 11 vols. (Lincoln: University of Nebraska Press, 2002-2003), 2:213.

10. Stephen E. Ambrose, *Undaunted Courage-Meriwether Lewis, Thomas Jefferson, and the Opening of the American West* (New York: Simon and Schuster, 1997), 85.

11. Carl P. Russell, *Guns On The Early Frontiers: A History of Firearms From Colonial Times Through The Years of the Western Fur Trade* (University of California Press, 1957), 177.

12. Jackson, 1:40.

13. Elliot Coues, ed., *The History of the Lewis and Clark Expedition* (New York: Francis P. Harper, 1883), 2:818-819.

14. Moulton, 6:442.

15. Flayderman, 440-41.

16. Kirk Olson, "A Lewis and Clark Rifle?," *American Rifleman* (May 1985), 24.

17. James E. Hicks, *U.S. Military Firearms 1776-1956* (La Canada, CA: James E. Hicks & Son, 1962), 14.

18. Flayderman, 497.

19. Jackson, 1:38-39.

20. Moulton, 3:349.

21. Jackson, 1:225.

22. Moulton, 4:300.

23. Ibid., 334.

24. Ibid., 299.

25. Jackson, 1:39.

26. Moulton, 4:369.

27. Ibid.

28. Ibid.

Chapter 4

Pennsylvania

Lancaster

After more than a month of preparations at Harper's Ferry, Lewis next traveled to Lancaster, Pennsylvania, arriving on 19 April 1803. He sought training from Andrew Ellicott, best known for conducting the initial survey for the establishment of Washington, DC, regarding the use of a sextant and chronometer. Mastering these scientific instruments would facilitate navigation and mapping.[1] Lewis' scientific training at Lancaster lasted for almost three weeks. Jefferson stated in his memoir of Lewis that he also attended to "the fabrication of the arms" while at Lancaster.[2] Jefferson is probably in error on this point. He might have transposed Harper's Ferry, the place where Lewis' weapons were being prepared, with the place where the weapons were originally constructed. If this is the case, Jefferson has unwittingly divulged the source of the contract rifles being modified at Harper's Ferry. The fact remains that no documents have been found, excluding Jefferson's memoir of Lewis, pointing to Lancaster as a source of weapons in addition to the 15 that were, by mid April 1803, being prepared at Harper's Ferry.

From Lancaster, Lewis reported to Jefferson that he had sent a flurry of letters to individuals residing on the frontier and in Philadelphia to make arrangements. One of these letters was addressed to an Indian interpreter Lewis sought to hire. Others provided the commanders of military posts along the Ohio and the Mississippi with his itinerary and requested their assistance in obtaining volunteers for his mission. Lewis, seeking to ensure the correct mix of skills among his men, made certain that volunteers were "to be engaged conditionally, or subject to [his] approval."[3] To get the construction of his keelboat under way, Lewis contacted William Dickson, a member of the House of Representatives from Nashville, Tennessee, to contract a boat builder on his behalf to "prepare a boat . . . as soon as possible, and to purchase a large light wooden canoe."[4] Finally, he wrote to General William Irvine, superintendent of military stores headquartered at Philadelphia, to assist him in procuring items "difficult to obtain, or may take the greates[t] length of time in their prepareation."[5]

On 7 May 1803, Ellicott wrote a letter to be carried by Lewis to Philadelphia for presentation to Robert Patterson, a professor of mathematics at the University of Pennsylvania and former president of the American Philosophical Society, who would provide Lewis additional advice and instruction regarding scientific instruments.[6] Lewis departed Lancaster sometime between 7 May and 14 May, setting off on a 10-hour trip over "the first extensive broken-stone highway in America, this original gravel road, 62 1/4 miles long, between Lancaster and Philadelphia, having been completed in 1795 at a cost of $465,000."[7]

Philadelphia

One historian has referred to Israel Whelan, America's purveyor of public supplies, as "the busiest man in Philadelphia" during Lewis' quest for supplies. Before Lewis arrived in Philadelphia, Whelan had received a directive and a draft for $1,000 from the secretary of war requesting his assistance in outfitting the expedition.[8] "From early May until mid-June, Whelan worked overtime, visiting retail and wholesale establishments where he purchased, from a list supplied by Lewis, a total of more than 200 different articles."[9] Lewis would also rely heavily on the equipment stores of the Schuylkill Arsenal commanded by General Irvine, whom Lewis had already forwarded a list of critical supplies. Armed with his recent scientific training, the support of the secretary of war, and the aid of Whelan, Lewis would scour local businesses and the arsenal in search of the items on his list.

The following sections provide brief discussions regarding the supplies obtained by Lewis. Items are categorized according to Lewis' List of Requirements (found at Appendix B) and a recapitulation of supplies actually obtained in Philadelphia (found at Appendix C). The medical aspects of the expedition are amplified in Appendices D, E, and F. Since the success of the expedition would ultimately depend on the establishment of friendly relations with the natives encountered along the route, it is appropriate to focus our attention on items intended for native consumption.

Indian Presents

Diplomacy with native tribes was predictably an essential aspect of the expedition. Jefferson, whose long-term goal was western expansion, recognized that the strategy most likely to achieve this aim was trade. Through gifts of diplomacy Lewis would display the quality and quantity of trade goods available from the United States. While doing so he hoped to thwart British and Spanish influence in the region by offering the potential for a steady supply of superior trade goods. Jefferson's vision included a network of trading posts radiating westward from the Mississippi. To support his vision he directed Lewis to confer with Indians on "the points most convenient" for these "emporiums" as well as "the articles of most desirable interchange for them and us."[10]

By the dawn of the 19th century, it had become an accepted and expected part of Indian diplomacy to "exchange gifts at each meeting."[11]

> French and English forest diplomats learned . . . to offer goods of substance and quality. While some Europeans may have perceived those gifts as bribes to ensure compliance with treaty terms, heaps of blankets, pots, and guns meant something else to the Indians. In the act of reciprocal gift giving, different peoples symbolized their concern for each other. Neglecting to give gifts meant failure to 'brighten the chain of friendship' that bound Europeans and Indians.[12]

Lewis, while aware of the president's long-term strategy, realized that a robust supply of trade goods would permit bartering for provisions, information, and means of transport from natives. He undoubtedly devoted a significant amount of time attempting to discern the mix of trade goods that would offer the best potential for bartering his group out of incalculable predicaments.

The sheer quantity of items is impressive. Of the eight categories of supplies assembled at Philadelphia, he paid out nearly a third of the almost $2,200 expended there on Indian presents. The final list of Indian presents included such items as almost 5,000 assorted needles; 3,000 fishhooks; 5,000 pocket looking glasses; 43 nesting brass kettles; and 10 pounds of nails. The list was designed to show off the array of trade goods available from American merchants. While Lewis' store of trade goods included many ornamental brooches and other luxury items, it also contained a large collection of items intended to improve native quality of life by making routine laborious tasks easier.

Two types of Indian presents, usually offered to Indian chiefs, are noticeably absent from Lewis' list. This is probably due to the fact that peace medallions and American flags were acquired in Washington before departing for Pennsylvania. Additional flags would be purchased at St. Louis. "The custom of presenting medals bearing the reigning sovereign's image to Indian chiefs was one long followed by European powers. United States medals bore the portrait of the current president. Jefferson medals came in three sizes with the same basic design; 105 mm (the largest ever issued), 76 mm, and 55 mm."[13] Lewis had two other varieties of medals in his possession as he headed west: a supply of medals bearing George Washington's portrait that measured 45 mm in diameter, which had been ordered during Washington's administration but received during Adams', and an often-overlooked stock of American Dollar coins configured to be presented as medals. Clark records on 29 October 1804: presented a "Cheaf [with] a Dollar of the American Coin as a Meadel with which he was much pleased."[14] Both flags and medals were offered to influential chiefs to establish a link between them and the United States government. An additional benefit of providing these symbols was that they conveyed a powerful admonition to European traders.

While the captains did trade with the Mandans and Hidatsas and other local tribes (mostly in the form of peace medals, flags, and tobacco) during their winter at Fort Mandan, they had little reason to dig deeply into their store of Indian presents. Lewis reported to Jefferson that he and his men had been able to subsist principally on meat obtained with their firearms and had maintained a large stock of the parched meal, as well as "portable soup, and a considerable proportion of pork and flour, which [he] intended for the more difficult parts of [their] voyage."[15] Clark, in undated field notes penned prior to departure up the Missouri in the spring of 1805, noted "We by the aide of our Black smiths procured Corn Sufficient for the party during the winter and about 70 or so bushels to Carry with us."[16]

By the time Lewis arrived in the vicinity of the Shoshones, he was prepared to open his stores to secure much-needed horses to traverse the Rockies. What the Shoshones desired most were guns, a commodity that the expedition was not in the position to trade. The Shoshones had previously dealt with Spanish traders and possessed horses with Spanish brands. Their predicament was that the "Spanish followed a fairly consistent policy of refusing to trade guns to Indians, in contrast to the French, English, and Americans. Having no direct contact with the Canadian or Missouri River trade systems, the Shoshones were at a great disadvantage, compared to their Blackfeet, Atsina, and Hidatsa enemies in obtaining firearms."[17]

Lewis and Clark opted to display the variety of trade goods in their possession, while promising that if their journey was successful that American traders would provide them with firearms. On 17 August 1805, Lewis recorded the following presentations to Shoshone chiefs:

> We gave the 1st Chief an uniform coat shi[rt] a pair of scarlet leggings a carrot of tobacco and some small articles to each of the others we gave a shi[r]t legging handkerchief a knife some tobacco and a few small articles we also distributed a good quantity paint mockerson awls knives beads lookingglasses &c among the other Indians.[18]

On 29 August 1805, Clark, seeking to build rapport with the Shoshones by demonstrating his commitment to providing his tribe with firearms, offered his Horseman's Pistol with ammunition in trade. The following day one of the men traded his musket for an additional horse. [19] The captains' diplomacy was successful; in addition to obtaining the approximately 40 desperately needed horses, they had also gained valuable allies. Lewis aptly summed up his feelings regarding the relationship when he noted on 17 August 1805 that "the chief thanked us for friendship towards himself and nation & declared his wish to serve us in every rispect; that he was sorry to find that it must yet be some time before they could be furnished with firearms but said they could live as they had done heretofore until we brought them as we had promised." [20]

After exiting the Rockies with the majority of its members undernourished and ill, the expedition's stock of trade goods would again be vital to securing much-needed provisions. On 11 October 1805, the party "halted at an Indian Lodge, to purchase provisions," which consisted of roots, "five dogs and a few fish dried." [21] By the expedition's arrival at the Pacific, expedition members would trade for more than 100 dogs to augment their diet.

On 19 January 1806, on the return trip, Lewis expended the last of his blue beads. While preparing for the expedition in Philadelphia, he noted on his list of requirements that blue beads are "far more valued than the white beads of the same manufacture and answers all the purposes of money." [22] Lewis would regret underestimating the quantity of blue beads he would need. While among the Chopunnish in May 1806 and running low on trade goods, Lewis noted that "blue beads however may form an exception to this remark; this article among all the nations of this country may be justly compared to goald or silver among civilized nations." [23] To show their good will and to once again secure the required number of horses required to cross the Rockies, Lewis presented the Chopunnish chief, Twisted Hair, a vial of "eye water" and "one gun and a hundred balls and 2 lbs. of powder in part for his attention to our horses and promised the other gun and a similar quantity of powder and lead when we received the balance of our horses." [24] Lewis did not, however, share with the chief that he had purchased the low-quality weapon from natives below on the river for two elk skins.

By the first days of June 1806, the expedition's supply of trade items was nearly exhausted. "High prices, accidents, and continued poor hunting made business With the Nez Perces increasingly difficult and jeopardized the explorers along the Lolo Trail." [25] By Clark's own admission the party had resorted to "every Subterfuge to prepare in the most ample manner in our power to meet that wretched portion of our journey, the Rocky Mountains."[26] To overcome their shortage of trade goods, the captains and their men began to improvise. In anticipation of the return crossing of the Rocky Mountains, the party traded buttons cut from the officers' coats, bits of metal fashioned into trinkets, and several medicinal concoctions to obtain a much-needed supply of roots and bread. On 6 June 1806, Clark declared victory by noting "The men who accompanied me obtained a good Store of roots and bread in exchange for a number of little notions, using the Yanke phrase, with which their own enginuiety had principally furnished them. On examonation we find our whole party have a Sufficient Store of bread and roots for our Voyage. A Circumstance not unpleasing."[27]

Lewis' relatively accurate estimate of necessary Indian presents enabled the expedition to gain rapport with the tribes along its westward route of travel and helped to secure provisions during the more arduous phases of the journey. The success of Lewis and Clark's frontier diplomacy on the westward journey enabled the acquisition of needed items from native tribes at reduced rates during the expeditions return trip, when the party's supplies were dwindling. If an urgent situation arose, the expedition possessed a large quantity of camp equipment that could also be used for barter.

Camp Equipage

Under the heading of "Camp Equipage," Lewis listed items such as tents, bags to move and store tools and equipment, cookware and eating utensils, sealing wax, and, arguably his most important items—six inkstands, six papers of ink powder, and 100 quills. Surely Lewis anticipated that only the most durable items of equipment would survive the journey. In his instructions Jefferson stated that upon reaching the Pacific, expedition members "will be without money, clothes or provisions" and suggested the use of credit to obtain replacements.[28]

In June 1803, while in Philadelphia, Lewis directed the fabrication of oiled linen cloth that could be used alternatively as tents, sails, or boat covers. He requisitioned shelter sections 5 feet wide and "rather more than 14 feet in length." When completed the shelter halves measured only 10 feet by 5 feet but apparently served their purpose. Two sections could be fastened together "to form two half faced Tents or Shelters Contrived in such manner their parts may be taken to pieces & again connected."[29] In conjunction with the order to fabricate the tent halves, Lewis also ordered the fabrication of 45 bags constructed of oiled linen. Each bag was numbered to allow for ease of inventory. The bags and the tent sections were made out of oiled linen to protect their contents from moisture. In addition to Lewis' custom-made tents, he received one common tent from Army stores.

It appears that Lewis' tents held up well east of the Rockies. On Saturday, 17 August 1805, he noted that after unloading their canoes and arranging their baggage on shore, the men "formed a canopy of one of our large sails and planted some willow brush in the ground to form a shade for the Indians to set under while we spoke to them."[30] By November, after traversing the mountains and enduring nonstop rain on the Pacific coast, Clark bleakly reported that he and the entire party "are all wet bedding and Stores, having nothing to keep our Selves or Stores dry, our [Indian] Lodge nearly worn out, and the pieces of Sales & tents So full of holes & rotten that they will not keep any thing dry."[31]

Prior to departing Camp Dubois, the expedition's permanent party, those who would travel to the Pacific and back, were organized into three squads. Each squad was further divided into two messes, groups that cook and share meals together. On 1 April 1804, Clark ordered that cooking and eating utensils be evenly distributed among the squads.[32] This system of messing remained in place for the duration of the expedition. No shortage of cookware or utensils is noted in the journals. However, due to the necessity of having to resort to using squad cookware as trade goods, and due to some petty theft by natives demonstrating a particular keenness for spoons, equipment must have been redistributed.

Lewis also correctly predicted the need to defend against mosquitoes, although he perceived them to be more of a nuisance than a potential disease vector. He thoughtfully acquired 11 mosquito curtains and ensured an ample supply of hog's lard. When smeared on the skin, the lard was supposed to ward off mosquitoes.[33] Much like today's insect repellant, it proved remarkably ineffective. Expedition journalists regularly concluded their daily entries by noting that "musquitors [were] verry troublesome this evening."[34] Lewis' mosquito nets and hog's lard may have missed the mark, but he compensated for it with his selection of tools.

The multiplicity of tools selected for the expedition is surprising considering their weight and the fact that Lewis' plan did not include the use of the keelboat beyond the Mandan Villages. While a significant quantity of tools was cached at the base of the Great Falls (a complete list of caches is found at Appendix I), many of the expedition's saws, shears, chisels, and adzes were transported by dugout canoe to the Pacific and back again. Expedition tools, in the hands of skilled, specially selected soldiers, enabled the construction of two fairly complex forts and more than a dozen canoes carved from logs.

To the historian, three items on Lewis' "Camp Equipage" receipt outshine the others. Lewis' 100 quills, six inkstands and six "papers" of ink powder enabled the party's busy pens to create the region's first accurate maps and to record "descriptions and precise illustrations of 122 species and subspecies of vertebrate animals and of 178 plants never previously described."[35] Without an adequate supply of these three relatively simple items, obtained from government stores, we would not have the American masterpiece assembled from nearly two million words recorded in expedition journals. [36]

Provisions &c

Many times during the journey, the Corps of Discovery went hungry for lack of adequate game or forage.[37] After painstakingly collecting the 40 horses required to haul their baggage westward over the grossly underestimated obstacle presented by the Rocky Mountains, the party set off. Lacking game and without the ability to barter with natives, Lewis' portable soup rapidly surpassed arms and ammunition in importance. On 16 September 1805, Sergeant Gass, one of the party's three noncommissioned officers, logged the fact that the expedition departed its camp early "and proceeded over the most terrible mountains" he had ever seen. During this daunting phase of the operation, Lewis' portable soup and their horses were their only source of food.

In his book *Only One Man Died: The Medical Aspects of the Lewis and Clark Expedition,* Dr. Eldon G. Chuinard asserts that "the most reliable experts of his time convinced him [Lewis] that portable soup, what we would call canned soup today, was the most reliable and nourishing article, as necessary for the success of the expedition as life itself."[38] It is produced by "long boiling evaporated the most cutrescent parts of the meat, [it] is reduced to the consistency of a glue, which in effect it is, and will like other glues, in a dry place, keep sound for years together."[39] Not a very appetizing description. It is obvious from the journals that the captains and their men did not relish their soup. On 16 September 1805, Sergeant Ordway recorded "we all being hungry and nothing to eat except a little portable soup which kept us verry weak, we killed another colt & eat half of it."[40] On 18 September 1805, Clark made a remarkably similar journal entry: "We dined & supped on a slant proportion of portable soupe, a few canesters of which, a little bears oil and about 20 lbs. Of candles form our stock of provision, the only recources being our guns & packhorses."[41]

Many historians misinterpret Clark's allusion to the expedition's 20 pounds of candles to infer that they were reduced to eating candles. While a dramatic touch, it is simply not true. None of the party's half-dozen journalists report the consumption of candles. Ordway and Clark both mention the slaughtering of colts to subsist. Ordway's entry implies that they only consumed half of the colt killed that day. While not intending to make light of the hunger endured during this most difficult phase of the expedition, it is far more likely that their hunger was induced by the miserable living conditions caused by an early winter storm, coupled with their desire to complete the passage as quickly as possible. Probably the best proof that the corps did not approach starvation at any time during the expedition can be found in Lewis' 24 May 1806 journal entry: "We are at a loss what to do for this unfortunate man [an ill native]. We gave him a few drops of Laudanum and a little portable soup."[42] It should be noted that this entry was made during their return trip, months after their westward crossing of the Rockies and after enduring a cold damp winter at Fort Clatsop, where at times game also proved scarce.

In addition to Lewis' portable soup, we find a number of other items under the heading of "Provisions &c" required to outfit 15 men. Thirty gallons of wine, (for medicinal purposes of course), shirts and "coatees" were purchased from local merchants. Lewis also obtained items regularly issued to Army soldiers and units from public stores, including watch coats, frocks, wool overalls, still more shirts and shoes.

The "coatees," made by Philadelphia tailor Francis Brown, offer another example of innovation and illustrate the nonstandard nature of the expedition's mission. On 6 June 1803, Lewis delivered material and presumably "verbally described the sort of thing he had in mind."[43] It appears that he intended to provide a sturdy jacket to expedition participants who had not previously served in the Army. In his pamphlet "Uniforms of the Lewis and Clark Expedition," Stephen Allie points out that "the pattern for the standard coat of the time would not fit on the allotted cloth. Nor would the pattern for a shorter coatee that was in design at the time and adopted in 1804. What could be cut was a double-breasted jacket of the sort referred to in the period as a roundabout."[44]

> The recruit coatees were made from super fine milled drab cloth. Super fine was a very high quality woolen cloth with a tight weave and heavily felted surface nap. The goods were so tight that exposed cut edges could be used without risk that the material would unravel. It was used for the very best civilian coats and officers' uniform coats. As such it was much superior to the woolen cloth used for enlisted men's coats by the Army. The term drab refers to a range of color between light gray and medium brown.[45]

Allie also provides insight into the selection of the 15 watch coats. "Every man of the 1st Infantry [Lewis' regiment] was provided with a blanket coat per the regimental standing orders of 1802."[46] However, Lewis expected that individuals recruited to join the expedition, not already serving in the Army, would benefit from the heavy watch coats that were "made of drab melton wool and were cut to restrict movement and maximize warmth."[47]

The journals offer many examples of members of the Corps of Discovery constructing clothing of hide to replace garments shredded by heavy labor or rotted by constant dampness. However, it is entirely likely that the captains possessed an adequate supply of even their most formal uniforms to "make a good showing to those that they might meet while in a diplomatic role."[48]

Mathematical Instruments

Jefferson's instructions specified that beginning at the mouth of the Missouri Lewis was to "take observations of latitude & longitude with great pains & accuracy, to be entered distinctly & intelligibly for others as well as yourself, to comprehend all the elements necessary."[49] The task of obtaining these observations required an array of scientific instruments. Having already spent three weeks training to use the sextant and the chronometer with Andrew Ellicott in Lancaster and receiving additional scientific training from Jefferson's associates, Robert Patterson and Dr. Benjamin Smith Barton, he possessed the knowledge necessary to purchase his instruments.

Upon reaching Philadelphia, Lewis immediately set out to obtain the instruments on his list of requirements. If price can be used as a measure of relative importance, the scientific equipment acquired in Philadelphia was the second most important category of supply. Two Philadelphia merchants received a total of $412.95 for a chronometer, sextant, quadrant, six compasses (see Figure 10), and other ancillary equipment required to obtain accurate celestial observations. Of these instruments, the most important were the chronometer, sextant, quadrant, three artificial horizons, and a circumferentor.[50]

At over $250, the chronometer was the most expensive item purchased for the expedition, except possibly the expedition's keelboat, for which no receipt has been found. A chronometer is a "clock of unusually fine construction, designed for extreme accuracy and dependability and built to withstand shock, vibration, and variations of temperature."[51] Without the ability to correlate an accurate time, provided by a chronometer, to a sighting of a celestial body, taken with a sextant or quadrant, it would be impossible to accurately track the expedition's westward progress, or longitude. In fact, for centuries it was exceptionally difficult for seafarers to accurately fix their east-west location on the earth's network of meridians and parallels for want of accurate timepieces. Thus, the simplest method of determining longitude requires a sextant or quadrant and a chronometer set to Greenwich time.[52]

Figure 10. Corps of Discovery compass and carrying case

After purchasing the chronometer, Lewis sent it to his instructor, Andrew Elliot, in Lancaster to examine and adjust. He enclosed the following note:

> I have at length been enabled to procure a Chronometer which you will receive by the hands of Mr. Barton who has been so obliging as take charge of her, you will also receive with her a screw driver and kee, the in[n]er cases of the Chronometer are confined by a screw. She is wound up and the works are stoped by inscerting a hog's bristle which you will discover by examineation. She has been cleaned by Mr. Voit, and her rate of going ascertained by observation to be 14" too slow in 24 h.[53]

The fact that the instrument proved to be 14 seconds slow during a 24-hour period proved to be of less consequence than the fact that both Lewis and Clark frequently forgot to wind it.[54]

37

Two instruments for sighting celestial bodies, a sextant and a quadrant, were also purchased in Philadelphia. Lewis and Clark, however, frequently refer to their octant as a "tangent screw quadrant." In any event, a sextant and an octant perform principally the same function. The difference between the two is that an octant, consisting of one-eighth of a circle, is capable of measuring 90 degrees of elevation, while a sextant, consisting of one-sixth of a circle, is capable of measuring 120 degrees of elevation. Coincidently, a quadrant, invented in 1711 and a precursor of the octant, is also capable of determining 90 degrees of elevation.[55] The additional elevation, or altitude attainable by a sextant, makes it ideal for lunar distance observations, while the octant "is ideally suited for observations of celestial bodies above the horizon."[56] Lewis' sextant was made of metal and came with three eyepieces. By sighting the horizon through the instrument's eyepiece while aligning it with a celestial body, he could measure the body's altitude by doubling the reading provided on the instrument's graduated arm.

On 22 July 1804, Lewis reported proudly that the "sun's altitude at noon has been too great to be reached with my sextant, for this purpose I have therefore employed the Octant by the back observation."[57] As previously stated, the maximum altitude measurable with a sextant is 120 degrees. This is accomplished by simply obtaining a maximum reading of 60 degrees on the graduated arm and doubling it. However, when the sun's angle above the horizon in the vicinity of Camp Dubois in July exceeded 60 degrees, doubling this measurement would exceed the capability of a sextant. Luckily, Lewis and his mentors anticipated this limitation and ensured that the expedition was armed with an octant configured to perform back observations. Lewis explains the technique used to obtain a back observation this way:

> The sun's altitude by the back observation express only the angle given by the graduated limb of the instrument at the time of observation, and are the complyment of the double Altitude of the sun's observed limb; if therefore the angle recorded be taken from 180° the remainder will be the double altitude of the observed object, or that which would be given by the fore observation with a reflecting surface.[58]

Lewis was also trained to employ three types of artificial horizon for use when the true horizon is obscured, as is often the case when navigating on land. The simplest form of artificial horizon proved to be Lewis' favorite. It used water as a reflecting surface when there was sufficient sunlight. The second consisted of a flat plane of glass "cemented" to a wooden ball. The third, formed out of a sextant mirror, was preferred when conducting night observations.[59]

One of the six compasses acquired by Lewis in Philadelphia was a circumferentor. The circumferentor was 6 inches in diameter and was used in conjunction with a level "to determine bearings and courses in mapping and to find 'the magnetic azimuth of the sun and pole star.'"[60]

Lewis' initial list of requirements included several items that are noticeably absent from the list of scientific equipment acquired in Philadelphia. The missing equipment includes three thermometers, a brass scale, two hydrometers, a theodolite, and a set of planispheres.

We know that Lewis acquired thermometers prior to departing from Pittsburgh because of the regular journal entries noting air and water temperature readings. These readings ended on 3 September 1805, when Clark reported a "great misfortune" in that their last thermometer was broken in an accident.[61] The brass scale was procured in Philadelphia and is accounted for under the heading of Camp Equipage. The hydrometers were apparently deemed to be unnecessary, for their use is not mentioned in the journals, nor is their absence lamented at any time during the journey. The "requisite [scientific] tables" might have included the planispheres, a device with which celestial bodies and dates can be correlated to create a representation of the night sky for a given date, or might have substituted for them. After consultation with his scientific mentors, Lewis reported to President Jefferson that Mr. Patterson and Mr. Ellicott both

> disapprove of the Theodolite as applicable to my purposes; they think it a delicate instrument, difficult of transportation, and one that would be very liable to get out of order; they also state that in it's application to any observations for obtaining the Longitude, it would be liable to many objections, and to much more inaccuracy than the Sextant.[62]

Lewis' only regret, in regard to scientific equipment, was the loss of his most fragile pieces of equipment, his thermometers. All measurements and observations requested by Jefferson, Patterson, and Ellicott were noted in the expedition's journals. However, the accuracy of the expedition's celestial observations was considerably degraded by Lewis and Clark's failure to wind the chronometer.

Arms & Accoutrements & Ammunition

While Lewis' 15 1792 contract rifles were being modified to his specifications at Harper's Ferry, he sought additional arms, as well as ammunition, in Philadelphia. On 18 May 1803, Lewis acquired two "Horseman's Pistols" from the Philadelphia Arsenal. Historians generally agree that the weapons provided were U.S. Model 1799 Flintlock Pistols that were patterned after France's Model 1777. Lewis' plan was to provide himself and the expedition's other officer (Clark's letter of acceptance had yet to be received) with "the convenience and 'insurance' provided by a small pocket weapon."[63] Model 1799 Flintlock Pistols were manufactured between 1799 and 1802 in Berlin, Connecticut.[64] They were .69 caliber, had a smoothbore 8 ½-inch barrel, and an overall length of 14 1/2 inches.[65] While the weapon's overall length seems large by modern standards, Lewis carried the weapon as part of his daily uniform. Although the Horseman's Pistols are sparingly mentioned in the expedition's journals, two entries support the contention that Lewis routinely carried his Horseman's Pistol during the entire expedition.

On 27 July 1806, while the expedition was on its return trip and was split into two separate parties, one led by Lewis exploring the Marias River, the other led by Clark exploring the Yellowstone River, Lewis drew his pistol in anger. After having been betrayed by a party of Blackfeet Indians he had been cautiously sharing a camp with, Lewis and his men were attacked. As he and his men grappled with the Indians for control of their guns, Lewis states that he "drew a pistol from my holster and terning myself about saw the Indian making off with my gun I ran at him with my pistol and bid him lay down my gun."[66]

Approximately two weeks later, Lewis again relied on his pistol for security. On 11 August 1806, he was accidentally shot by one of his men while hunting. In the initial confusion Lewis thought he was under attack by natives, which is entirely understandable considering his earlier confrontation with the Blackfeet. After hobbling back to a pirogue with a painful thigh wound, Lewis recorded that he prepared himself with a pistol, a rifle, and his air gun "being determined as a retreat was impracticable to sell my life as deerly as possible."[67]

Clark, on the other hand, was less attached to his Horseman's Pistol and retained it only until the fall of 1805. On 16 November 1804, while enduring a well-provisioned winter at the Mandan Villages, Clark was approached by "an old man [who] came looking for a pistol in return for some corn and four buffalo robes."[68] Clark rejected the offer because, having just completed what he anticipated as the easiest leg of their journey to the Pacific, he perceived the trade to be lopsided. It would not be until August 1805, when the Rockies loomed large and the expedition critically needed to win over the Shoshone to secure the horses and guides required to cross the mountains, did Clark note in his journal, "I purchased a horse for which I gave my Pistol 100 Balls Powder & a Knife."[69]

In addition to the Horseman's Pistols, on 7 June 1803, Lewis secured an additional pair of pistols for $10.00 from Philadelphia merchant Robert Barnhill. Little is known about this second pair of pocket pistols. They were apparently smaller than the Horseman's Pistols, and the fact that they had "secret triggers" implies that their small size required some type of nonstandard trigger mechanism. Only a single journal entry mentions their potential use. On 30 March 1804, Clark wrote, in a particularly illegible journal entry, that he has loaded "a small pair of pistols" in anticipation of "inforcing our regulation." It would appear that Clark expected "some trouble with the men, either over the announcement of the verdict of the court-martial or over the stealing of goods from the supplies due to be delivered that evening."[70] Trouble failed to materialize and the pistols were not required.

One of Lewis' most interesting innovations related to the storage of two critical commodities, lead and powder. Lewis' challenge was to craft a means of transporting the 176 pounds of powder and 420 pounds of lead, obtained in Philadelphia, over rough terrain and varied weather conditions that would be encountered on the journey.

Innovation was essential because expedition members would find it difficult to keep the contents of conventional ammunition containers dry. Lewis knew that he and his soldiers would be operating in a continually damp environment. He also knew that the canisters routinely provided by powder manufacturers were convenient but lacked the durability required for a lengthy operation. What he needed was a method to store bulk powder that would prove sturdier than the 6 ¼-pound wooden kegs used by powder manufacturers.[71]

Lewis developed a canister constructed out of 8 pounds of lead capable of containing 4 pounds of powder. The canisters had narrow mouths that were corked, then sealed with wax to limit exposure to moisture. These compact containers were designed to refill the individual powder horns carried by soldiers. When empty, the containers would then be melted and formed into balls. The number of balls formed by an empty canister was proportional to the powder dispensed. The general rule of thumb was "3 grains weight of powder for each 7 grains weight of ball."[72] On 1 February 1806, while at the expedition's wintering post and after having completed the most difficult part of their journey, Clark recorded:

To day we opened and examined all our Ammunition, which has been Secured in leaden Canistirs. we found twenty Sevin of the best Rifle powder, 4 of Common rifle, 3 of Glaize and one of Musquet powder in good order, perfectly as dry as when first put in the Canisters, although the whole of it from various accidince have been for hours under the water, these Cannisters Contain 4 pounds of powder each and 8 of Lead. had it not been for that happy expedient which Capt Lewis devised of Securing the powder by means of the Lead, we Should have found great dificuelty in keeping dry powder un till this time.[73]

The 52 leaden canisters that Lewis had fabricated in Philadelphia ensured that expedition members would never lack powder or lead.

Using the 3:7 ratio of powder to ball noted above, the 176 pounds of powder and 420 pounds of lead acquired in Philadelphia equates to approximately a 2.93:7 ratio. This ratio would enable expedition weapons to fire more than 11,700 rounds, assuming an average weapon caliber of .55 at 28 balls per pound of lead. Lewis procured more than four times the powder and ball that would have actually been expended by a 15-man outfit. Even when the corps expanded to over 30 in the permanent party, expedition members still had an ample supply of powder and lead.

To ensure that they would not want for flints, Lewis picked up 500 rifle flints and 125 musket flints. Based on the assumption that he based his requirement for 500 rifle flints on the anticipated usage of his fifteen rifles being prepared at Harper's Ferry, he apparently expected to have at least four muskets along for the journey as well. According to the Ordnance Manual of 1841, good quality flints would last approximately 50 firings but were issued to soldiers at the rate of one flint for every 20 balls.[74] Based on the number of flints acquired, and assuming a conservative expenditure of one flint per 30 rounds fired, Lewis had the flint capacity to fire approximately 18,750 rounds. Using the even more conservative method of issue outlined in the 1841 Ordnance Manual, Lewis could count on the capability to fire 12,500 rounds with the flints in his possession, which is roughly in line with the 11,760-round supply of powder and ball cited above. The final number of muskets carried with the expedition's permanent party was probably closer to 15. The volunteers that joined from frontier garrisons probably arrived with muskets. It is likely that these men arrived with a supply of five flints each. It is also possible that additional flints were provided from garrison stocks or purchased in St. Louis.

Powder, ball, and flints were never in short supply. In fact, surplus powder and lead was cached on both sides of the Rockies (see Appendix I). As has been discussed, Lewis' limiting factor for the number of rounds his expedition was capable of firing was lead. He undoubtedly subscribed to the belief that the expedition could survive without many of the items on his packing list. However, quality weapons, adequate powder and lead, and an ample supply of flints were non-negotiable.

Medicines &c

The medical preparations conducted by Lewis in Pennsylvania warrant study, more for historical completeness than for any hope of contemporary relevance of the techniques, tools, and medicines used during the journey. In retrospect, little valuable therapy beyond the observation that narcotics effectively reduce pain can be learned. Certainly, Lewis and Clark built rapport with tribes by providing medical care to injured and sick natives.

One member of the expedition, Sergeant Charles Floyd, became ill and died approximately halfway between St. Louis and the Mandan Villages. It is generally acknowledged that he suffered a ruptured appendix. This condition would have proved fatal even if he were in Philadelphia, since the first successful appendectomy would not occur for over 80 years after Sergeant Floyd's illness. Ironically, it was Lewis, the expedition's trained medic, who suffered the most serious wound. On 11 August 1806, while leading a hunting party, a nearsighted subordinate shot him through the buttocks and thigh. He recorded in his journal that:

> A ball struck my left thye about an inch below my hip joint, missing the bone it passed through . . . the stroke was very severe . . . I took off my clothes and dressed my wounds . . . introducing tents of patent lint into the ball holes . . . I slept on board . . . the pain I experienced excited a high fever.[75]

His medical training and his supplies probably saved his life. Dr. Volney Steel, a pathologist and author of "Lewis and Clark Military Explorers, Scientists, and Physicians," estimates the expedition's medical capabilities this way:

> The two captains were as prepared as any "qualified" contemporary doctors to treat most of the common medical conditions of the frontier. The more common problems they expected to see included "turners" (tumors), "biles" (boils), "pox" (syphilis, also called Lues or French

Disease), "char lick" (colic), and "biliousness." Lewis and Clark had a rudimentary knowledge of surgery at a time when surgical procedures were restricted to the external surface of the body and the extremities . . . it is doubtful that they washed their hands or surgical instruments.[76]

Very little formal training existed for aspiring physicians in 1803. They were trained by means of an inconsistent apprenticeship system. The early 19th century offered "essentially . . . no opportunity for a medical education, no hospitals as we know them today, and no medical journals."[77] The first state to license medical doctors did not do so until 11 years after the expedition's return.

Having several family members—to include two daughters, his only son, and his wife—perish while under the care of physicians of questionable competence, Jefferson developed a skeptical view of doctors.[78] His general mistrust of medical personnel is illustrated by the following passage penned in June 1807:

> One of the most successful physicians I have ever known has assured me, that he used more bread pills, drops of colored water, and powders of hickory ashes, than of all other medicines put together. . . . That the inexperienced and presumptuous band of medical tyros let loose upon the world, destroys more of human life in one year, than all the Robinhoods, Cartouches, and Macheaths do in a century.[79]

Even so, Jefferson contacted his friend and Edinburgh-trained physician, Dr. Benjamin Rush (see Figure 11), to secure medical training at Philadelphia for Lewis.

Lewis' apprenticeship with Rush lasted about two weeks. In keeping with his thirst for scientific information, Jefferson requested that Rush provide Lewis with a list of questions intended to gain insight into native lifestyles. Rush's questions (the complete list can be found at Appendix E) ranged from inquiries about the age at which natives marry, to suicidal tendency and motivations.[80] Rush also provided Lewis with a list of rules to help preserve the health of expedition members during "laborious enterprises & marches"[81] (the complete list is found at Appendix D). His list proclaims the usefulness of resting in "a horizontal posture," the virtue of washing one's cold feet in alcohol, and purging by means of ingesting one or more of the expedition's stock of "Thunderclappers," pills personally formulated by Rush and selflessly sold to Lewis. The "purgative combination" used to concoct Rush's Thunderclappers "is not used today, and such a dosage would be considered quite heroic."[82] Most soldiers would not need to be coached to assume a "horizontal posture" after particularly difficult stretches of the journey. The journals record the fact that Lewis and Clark freely dispensed Rush's purging pills. However, it has so far proved impossible for historians to locate a single passage dedicated to the usefulness of applying the party's limited supply of spirits to cold feet!

Figure 11. Dr. Benjamin Rush

With the aid of Israel Whelan, Lewis purchased the expedition's medical supplies from Philadelphia druggists Gillaspay and Strong. When his shopping was complete, Lewis' new medicine chests were packed with cathartics intended to induce purging of intestines, emetics intended to induce vomiting, diuretics to increase production of urine, and lancets to aid in the removal of "excess" blood.

There were three major notions regarding the treatment of disease at the dawn of the 19th century. The first centered on nervous system stimulation, or lack thereof, as the cause of disease. To combat "excessive nervous stimulation," Lewis obtained a "half pound of the best Turkish opium as well as laudanum, an alcoholic tincture containing about 10 percent opium and certainly not of least importance wine and a supply of whiskey."[83] The second notion asserted that the key to health was maintaining the correct balance of bodily fluids. For instance, if a soldier became flushed, had a rapid heart beat, and felt weak after hauling a canoe several miles overland, it was probably the result of too much blood in the soldier's circulatory system. The remedy was to employ the medical kit's "best lancets" to remove the surplus blood. It is ironic that, at least initially, the soldier's blood pressure would undoubtedly drop, giving the appearance that excess blood was in fact the culprit rather than dehydration or other legitimate cause. The third concept hypothesized that "disease was either caused by or contributed to by poisons in the intestines."[84] Lewis' preferred method of combating these "poisons" was to liberally dispense one or more of the 600 Thunderclappers previously discussed.

In his book *Or Perish in the Attempt, Wilderness Medicine in the Lewis and Clark Expedition*, Dr. David Peck provides an excellent summary of some of the other medicines purchased by Lewis:

> The list included such herbal cathartics as powdered jalap and rhubarb. Other cathartic salts such as sodium sulfate, known as "Glauber's salts," and magnesia were purchased in the unlikely event that the jalap couldn't do the job. Various emetics (which produce vomiting) such as ipecacuan, and the antimony-potassium compound called tartar emetic were added to the medicine chest. Nutmeg, clove and cinnamon were purchased to flavor foul-tasting medicines as well as lessening the intestinal griping of some of the cathartics. Topical analgesics (pain relievers) such as gum camphor, tragacanth, and calamine ointment would help with skin problems.[85]

Peck and Dr. Chuinard are in agreement that the 15 pounds of Peruvian bark, the largest quantity and most expensive single item on Lewis' list of medicines (wine is listed under provisions), was one of the few "beneficial items Lewis purchased." The "barks" had been in use since the 17th century and were used effectively to combat the fever associated with malaria.[86]

Lewis, probably as a result of experience acquired during frontier service, assumed that his men would contract venereal disease. Several expedition members contracted the disease from Mandan and Clatsop women whose company was freely offered to expedition soldiers by their husbands. Native men sought to acquire the spiritual power of the white men by encouraging extramarital sexual relations with their wives. Such unions were also practiced between elderly warriors and the spouses of younger warriors.[87] Undoubtedly, expedition soldiers shared their spiritual power freely, as evidenced by numerous cases of syphilis requiring treatment. The most common treatment mentioned in expedition journals is that of the application of an ointment consisting primarily of mercury and applied directly to the lesion.[88] Lewis was also prepared to treat gonorrhea. His medicine chests contained four penile syringes designed to "inject standard urethral irrigations of the day," most likely "'balsam copaiba," an oily and acidic substance obtained from a South American tree.[89]

"Eye water" consisting of lead acetate and zinc sulfate, ingredients identified on Lewis' list of medicines as "Sacchar. Saturn. Opt." and ""Vitriol Alb.," respectively, was highly sought after by tribes west of the Rockies to soothe eyes damaged by constant dust and a poor diet. Administered primarily by Clark, the eye water, as previously mentioned, enabled the expedition, dangerously short of trade goods by the spring of 1806, to barter for provisions.

Lewis also acquired basic dentistry tools, basic surgical tools (probably to remove digits and to dress wounds), a grossly overpriced tourniquet and a single clyster (enema) syringe.[90] Probably in deference to modesty, expedition journals do not mention the use of either the penile syringes or the clyster syringe.

While Lewis had the benefit of the best medical advice available, "some credit must be given to simple luck. Fortunately, none of the voyagers contracted any of the killer diseases of the era, such as smallpox, yellow fever, malaria, cholera, or typhoid."[91] Although the expedition suffered the loss of Sergeant Floyd to a then-untreatable ailment, it is undeniable that Lewis and Clark successfully "treated" their men and scores of natives along their route.

After spending over a month receiving instruction regarding celestial navigation, botany, and medicine, as well as spending $2,160.14 on a critical mix of supplies and equipment to be consolidated at Harper's Ferry, Lewis returned to Washington for final preparations before setting off for his port of debarkation, Pittsburgh.

Pittsburgh

On 10 June 1803, Lewis corresponded with William Linnard, the military agent responsible for the transportation of military goods in the region, regarding the movement of his supplies from Harper's Ferry and Philadelphia to Pittsburgh. Lewis recommended a wagon drawn by a team of five horses to move his 3,500 pounds of equipment. On 5 July Lewis departed Washington, probably by way of Fredericksburg, Virginia, en route to Harper's Ferry. On 8 July he reported to Jefferson that Linnard's wagoner had arrived at Harper's Ferry on 28 June but had neglected to load the expedition's gear because "his team was not sufficiently strong to take the whole of the articles that had been prepared for me at this place and therefore took none of them."[92] After hastily coordinating transportation for his cargo, Lewis set off for Pittsburgh, arriving on 15 July.

He was instructed to meet with Lieutenant Moses Hooke, the commanding officer of Fort Fayette and the region's assistant military agent. During the first week of July, Secretary Dearborn had directed Hooke to "give Capt. Lewis every aid" within his power to ensure that his embarkation went smoothly and that the vessel for which Lewis had contracted was adequately provisioned to "carry him & his Men to [Fort] Massac." Fort Massac was located at the junction of the Ohio and Mississippi Rivers and would provide several members of the expedition's permanent party.

Hooke must have impressed Lewis. Lacking a reply from Clark as to whether he would participate in the journey, Lewis, on 26 July, informed Jefferson:

> In the event of Mr. Clark's declining to accompany me Lieut. Hooke of this place has engaged to do so, if permitted; and I think from his disposition and qualifications that I might safely calculate on being as ably assisted by him in the execution of the objects of my mission, as I could wish, or would be, by any other officer in the Army.[93]

Jefferson and Dearborn apparently endorsed Hooke's selection, with Dearborn directing on 3 August that Hooke get his accounts in order in anticipation of relinquishing his position to another officer.[94] All of this planning was for naught, for Clark on 18 July penned the following enthusiastic response to Lewis' invitation:

> The enterprise &c. is Such as I have long anticipated and am much pleased with-and as my situation in life will admit of my absence the length of time necessary to accomplish such an undertaking I will chearfully join you in an 'official Charrector' as mentioned in your letter.[95]

Lewis' response, dated 3 August, betrays his earlier comment that Hooke was as qualified as any officer in the Army to accompany him on the expedition:

> Be assured I feel myself much gratified with your decision; for I could neither hope, wish, or expect from a union with any man on earth, more perfect support or further aid in the discharge of the several duties of my mission, than that, which I am confident I shall derive from being associated with yourself.[96]

With Clark's acceptance denying him a prominent place in American history, Hooke dutifully aided Lewis' departure. Dearborn's initial correspondence to Hooke also directed him to provide 18 light axes, items that originally appeared on Lewis' list of requirements under the category of Indian presents and were to be received in Tennessee.[97]

Lewis' initial plan called for the overland movement of his cargo from Pennsylvania to Tennessee. On 20 April 1803, Lewis wrote to Dr. William Dickson, a member of the House of Representatives from Tennessee residing in Nashville, requesting that he expeditiously and confidentially contract with a boat builder for the construction of a vessel and for the purchase of a "large light wooden canoe."[98] By the time Lewis penned his invitation to Clark on 19 June, he had switched his point of embarkation to Pittsburgh, probably because Dickson was unable to secure a satisfactory contract.

Upon his arrival in Pittsburgh, Lewis reported to Jefferson that "all is well" regarding his preparations thus far. He stated that he had not yet inquired as to the status of his boat "on the state of which, the time" of his departure was dependant.[99] On 22 July he wrote to Jefferson to inform him that his supplies had arrived safely from Harper's Ferry and to report his first problems with the contractor constructing his boat. The boat was supposed to be complete by 20 July. The contractor reported that because of a shortage of timber, which he had overcome, he anticipated finishing the vessel by the end of the month. Like the savvy logistician he now was, Lewis added a week to the boat builder's estimate and reported to the president that it was his belief that the boat would not be ready prior to 5 August.

Lieutenant Hooke recorded Lewis' departure from Pittsburgh on 1 September. Lewis undoubtedly could not bring himself to explain his five-week delay to the president until his bow was oriented westward. It is impossible to more succinctly communicate the depth of Lewis' frustration with his boat contractor than is contained in his letter to Jefferson dated 8 September 1803:

> According to his usual custom he [the contractor] got drunk, quarreled with his workmen, and several of them left him, nor could they be prevailed on to return: I threatened him with the penalty of his contract, and exacted a promise of greater sobriety in future which, he took care to perform with as little good faith, as he had his previous promises with regard to the boat, continuing to be constantly either drunk or sick. I spent most of my time with the workmen, alternately presuading and threatening, but neither threats, persuasion or any other means which I could devise were sufficient to procure the completion of the work sooner than the 31st of August.[100]

In addition to a sketch contained in Clark's field notes, the expedition journals contain a considerable amount of information on the keelboat (see Figure 12) constructed by Lewis' less than sober boat contractor. We know that "She was 55 feet long with an 8-foot 4-inch beam and a 3-foot draft."[101] As the photos of a keelboat reproduction below illustrate, Lewis' boat resembled vessels widely used by the Spanish to patrol trade establishments along the Mississippi and Missouri Rivers.[102]

Figure 12. Keelboat reproduction. Source: Dr. Vince Gutowski.

The vessel could be propelled by three means: two sails (one mast would eventually be removed), 20 oars, and by a variable number of soldiers equipped with poles. It was not uncommon to employ two or more methods simultaneously.

By the time Lewis set off from Pittsburgh, the Ohio River's water level was so low that he was advised by individuals familiar with "the navigation of the river declared it impracticable to descend it."[103] The Ohio's shallow waters prompted Lewis to hire a pilot, and he opted to send the majority of his cargo overland to Wheeling, Virginia.[104] When traversing exceptionally difficult sections of river, the keelboat also employed oxen, horses, and men to tow it over sandbars and obstructions.

Although acutely aware of the dwindling season available to him as a result of delays at Harper's Ferry and Pittsburgh, he must have had a sense of accomplishment in the mass of supplies and equipment collected. His primary concern would now be meeting his dear friend, William Clark, near Louisville and the acquisition of the endeavor's most critical resource, the men that they would lead to the western ocean.

Notes

1. Paul R. Cutright, "Contributions of Philadelphia to Lewis and Clark History," *We Proceeded On*, supplementary publication no. 6 (July 1982), 2-3.

2. Elliot Coues, ed. *The History of the Lewis and Clark Expedition* (New York: Dover, 1950), 1:xxii.

3. Donald Jackson, ed., *Letters of the Lewis and Clark Expedition, with Related Documents: 1783-1854*, 2 vols., 2nd ed (Urbana: University of Illinois Press, 1978), 1:38.

4. Ibid.

5. Ibid.

6. Cutright, 5-6.

7. Ibid., 3.

8. Ibid., 15.

9. Ibid.

10. James P. Ronda, *Lewis and Clark Among the Indians* (Lincoln: University of Nebraska Press, 1984), 5.

11. Ronda, 8.

12. Ibid.

13. Gary E. Moulton, ed., *The Definitive Journals of Lewis and Clark*, 11 vols. (Lincoln: University of Nebraska Press, 2002-2003), 2: 443.

14. Moulton, 3:210.

15. Jackson, 1:234.

16. Moulton, 3:486.

17. Ibid., 5:95.

18. Ibid., 5:112.

19. Ibid., 5:178.

20. Ibid., 5:111.

21. Ibid., 5:262.

22. Jackson, 1:74.

23. Moulton, 7:252.

24. Ibid., 7:248.

25. Ronda, 229.

26. Moulton, 7:328.

27. Ibid., 7:342.

28. Jackson, 1:65.

29. Ibid., 1:71.

30. Moulton, 5:111.

31. Ibid., 6:91.

32. Ibid., 2:189.

33. David J. Peck, *Or Perish in the Attempt: Wilderness Medicine in the Lewis and Clark Expedition* (Helena, MT: Farcountry Press, 2002), 51.

34. Moulton, 4:418.

35. Volney Steele, "Lewis and Clark: Military Explorers, Scientists, and Physicians," *Military History of the West* (Fall 2001), 51.

36. Ruben Gold Thwaites, ed., *Original Journals of the Lewis and Clark Expedition* (New York: DSI Digital Reproduction, 2001), 1:xlv; Moulton, 2:40–42.

37. Carol L. MacGregor, ed. *The Journals of Patrick Gass: Member of the Lewis and Clark Expedition* (Missoula, MT: Mountain Press Publishing Company, 1997), 130.

38. Eldon G. Chuinard, *Only One Man Died: The Medical Aspects of the Lewis & Clark Expedition* (Fairfield, WA: Ye Galleon Press, 1998), 161.

39. Chuinard, 162.

40. Moulton, 9:225.

41. Ibid., 5:211.

42. Ibid., 7:284.

43. Stephen J. Allie, "The Uniforms of the Lewis and Clark Expedition," Frontier Army Museum. Fort Leavenworth, KS (Summer 2002), 5.

44. Ibid., 5.

45. Ibid., 5-6.

46. Ibid., 4.

47. Ibid.

48. Ibid., 2.

49. Jackson, 2:62.

50. Ibid., 1:82-88.

51. Edmond A Gibson, *Basic Seamanship and Navigation* (New York: McGraw- Hill, 1951), 276.

52. Per Collinder, *A History of Maritime Navigation* (New York: St. Martin's Press, 1955), 138.

53. Cutright, 7.

54. Moulton, 2:87.

55. Peter Ifland, "The History of the Sextant," Article available on-line. http://www.mat.uc.pt/~helios/Mestre/Novemb00/H61iflan.htm. Internet. Accessed 1 February 2003.

56. Ibid.

57. Moulton, 2:411.

58. Ibid.

59. Ibid., 2:412.

60. Ibid., 2:87.

61. Moulton, 5:186.

62. Jackson, 1:48.

63. Carl P. Russell, *Guns On The Early Frontiers: A History of Firearms From Colonial Times Through The Years of the Western Fur Trade* (Berkeley: University of California Press, 1957), 84.

64. Norm Flayderman, *Flayderman's Guide to Antique American Firearms ... and their values* (Northbrook, IL: DBI Books, 1994), 286.

65. Flayderman, 286.

66. Moulton, 8:134.

67. Ibid., 8:154.

68. Ronda, 102.

69. Moulton, 5:178.

70. Moulton, 2:183.

71. Russell, 227.

72. Russell, 231.

73. Moulton, 6:272.

74. Russell, 239.

75. Steele, 57.

76. Ibid., 51.

77. Chuinard, 62.

78. Cutright, 8.

79. Chuinard, 416.

80. Drake W. Will, "The Medical and Surgical Practice of the Lewis and Clark Expedition," *Journal of the History of Medicine and Allied Sciences* (Spring 1959), 276.

81. Will, 278.

82. Chuinard, 156.

83. Peck, 49.

84. Ibid., 51.

85. Ibid., 49.

86. Chuinard, 156-57; Peck, 49-50.

87. Moulton, 3:268.

88. Peck, 52.

89. Chuinard, 159.

90. Peck, 51.

91. Steele, 52-53.

92. Jackson, 1:106.

93. Ibid., 114.

94. Ibid., 115.

95. Ibid., 110.

96. Ibid., 115.

97. Ibid., 101.

98. Ibid., 40.

99. Ibid., 110.

100. Ibid., 121-22.

101. Richard C. Boss, "Keelboat, Pirogue, and Canoe: Vessels Used by the Lewis and Clark Corps of Discovery," *Nautical Research Journal* (June 1999), 69.

102. Russell, 255.

103. Ibid., 122.

104. Ibid., 121-22.

Chapter 5

Down the Ohio to Camp Dubois

Transportation

Lewis departed Pittsburgh on 31 August "with a party of 11 hands 7 of which are soldiers, a pilot and three young men on trial they having proposed to go with me throughout the voyage."[1] This small crew, only one man short of the number authorized by Congress, manned a pirogue and his recently constructed keelboat.

Lewis first revealed the presence of the pirogue on 4 September. The vessel was acquired to lighten the keelboat's load in hopes of overcoming the low water level of the Ohio River. The term *pirogue* refers to a "dugout canoe which was presumably shaped from a large log."[2] It is doubtful that Lewis was applying the term correctly. As was common at the time, the term pirogue was used to describe a "broad range of riverine craft."[3] This is illustrated by the fact that expedition journals alternate between the terms canoe and pirogue for any vessel smaller than the keelboat. Lewis displays the same flexibility when referring to the keelboat, periodically describing it as a boat, keelboat, or bateau. Further evidence that Lewis' pirogue was not a traditional log canoe is contained in Lewis' journal entry of 4 May 1805, in which he remarked, "we were detained this morning until about 9 Ock. In order to repare the rudder irons of the red perogue which were broken last evening in landing." And again on 5 May, he noted that "the rudder irons of both pirogues broke."[4]

It has been speculated that the bateau presents the best "example in terms of size, shape, and construction for the pirogues of the Corps of Discovery."[5] The word *bateau* merely means boat in French and was used about as broadly as boat is today. "However, early in the eighteenth century bateau became accepted as a name for a double ended, flat-bottomed, chine-built craft used extensively along the St. Lawrence River and on the American lakes. Colonial bateaux, used both commercially and militarily, were built up to 50 feet long, and were propelled primarily by rowing and poling."[6]

Even after taking the precaution of sending the majority of cargo by wagon to Wheeling, acquiring a pirogue to lighten the keelboat's load, and hiring an experienced river pilot to avoid the river's obstructions, Lewis still encountered great difficulty negotiating the Ohio. At one point he was forced to employ a team of oxen to augment the exertions of his crew to pass a particularly shallow section of river. On 8 September Lewis "purchased a [second] perogue and hired a man to work her"[7] to further distribute the weight of his heavier cargo loaded at Wheeling.

According to notes accompanying Clark's sketch of the smaller white pirogue, it was capable of hauling "8 Tuns." Based on complex calculations using the mass and dimensions of men and supplies, one historian estimates that the vessel must have been 39 feet long and had a beam of about 8 1/2 feet.[8] The red pirogue (see Figure 13), which "was propelled by only one additional oar . . . could not have been much larger."[9] It has further been

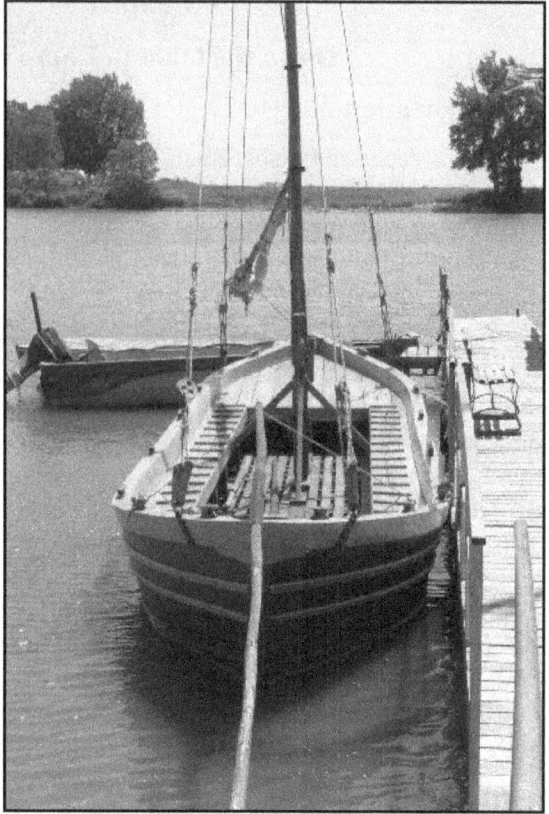

Figure 13. Red pirogue reproduction

Dr. Vince Gutowski

speculated that this larger pirogue was capable of hauling 9 tons plus the vessel's crew with its 41 ½-foot length and 9-foot beam.[10] With the addition of the second pirogue, the Corps of Discovery now had the capability to haul "29 tons with 12 tons in the keelboat, 9 tons in the red pirogue, and 8 tons in the white pirogue."[11] Even after making an allowance for the fact that the expedition's payload would decrease as it progressed westward, it still seemed beyond the capability of a mere dozen men to manhandle to the Pacific and back.

Personnel

While making final preparations in Washington during the first week of July 1803, Lewis consulted with Secretary Dearborn regarding expedition manning. Soon after their discussion Dearborn dispatched letters to Lewis and to three frontier commanders, Captains Russell Bissell, Amos

Stoddard, and Daniel Bissell. Dearborn's letter to Lewis offered Fort Massac, located on the lower Ohio, and Fort Kaskaskia, located on the Mississippi north of the mouth of the Ohio, as sources for expedition personnel. Dearborn reiterates to Lewis that he is limited to personnel of which "the whole number of non-commissioned officers and privates should not exceed twelve." [12] You will recall that Lewis' letter of invitation to Clark on 19 June also referenced these installations as a source of manpower. In Dearborn's correspondence to Russell Bissell and Amos Stoddard, we find the first reference to a personnel requirement beyond the 10 to 12 already authorized. His letter directed the captains to "furnish one Sergeant & Eight good Men who understand rowing a boat to go with Capt. Lewis as far up the River as they can go & return with certainty before the Ice will obstruct the passage of the river." [13] These nine men were intended to accompany the expedition only to the party's wintering site, presumably returning to their posts prior to the onset of winter. The exact mission of these troops is not described in the letter, but it appears they were intended to provide additional security to the party while negotiating territory controlled by Teton Sioux. It can also be assumed that Lewis, familiar with the hazards regularly encountered by traders negotiating Sioux lands, asked Dearborn for a security party while in Washington. This fact is significant because it illuminates the fact that Lewis was already experiencing misgivings about the small size of his party and begins to explain why the number in his party more than tripled its authorized strength prior to departing Camp Dubois.

On 3 August 1803, Lewis, in his letter acknowledging receipt of Clark's acceptance of his offer of co-command, emphasized that the nature of their enterprise depended on the careful selection of the men, "their qualifications should be such as perfectly fit them for the service, outherwise they will reather clog than further the objects in view." [14] Although it is impossible to precisely determine who of the expedition's permanent party departed Pittsburgh on board the keelboat, several historians propose that the expedition's youngest member, George Shannon, and John Colter were the first to demonstrate that they had the right stuff. [15] After consuming four difficult weeks hauling the keelboat over the obstacles, then enjoying a week's sabbatical studying fossil remains at Big Bone Lick at the request of President Jefferson, Lewis arrived at Clarksville, Indiana Territory on 15 October. [16] Clark doubtlessly greeted his friend warmly. Lewis must have been relieved to see that seven able woodsmen accompanied him (for a complete list of personnel, see Appendix G). Clark's seven men plus, most probably, Shannon and Colter, would go down in history as the "nine young men from Kentucky."[17] But the most important addition to the party was William Clark.

As previously discussed, the president authorized Lewis to secure the services of an additional officer. With Jefferson's assistance Lewis sought a captain's commission to reinforce their parity. For reasons almost certainly related to the Army's significant drawdown of 1802, Clark received a lieutenant's commission in the Corps of Artillerists.[18] On having to share this awkward revelation with Clark, Lewis exclaimed, "it is not such as I wished, or had reason to expect; but so it is—a further explaneation when I join you. I think it will be best to let none of our party or any other persons know any thing about the grade, you will observe that the grade has no effect upon your compensation, which by G--d, shall be equal to my own."[19] Lewis lived up to his promise, selflessly shared his authority and gratefully spread the weight of command. Both officers protected Clark's true rank from the men.[20] Lewis accurately surmised that Clark's talents and abilities would perfectly complement his own. His depth of emotion and unambiguous concern for his men, as well as the Indians, along the expedition's route saturates his prose. It is he who declared "Ocian in View!" on 7 November 1805, and "Oh! How Horriable is the Day!" eight sodden days later. Combining their efforts the captains would spend the next seven months collecting more supplies and searching for additional "good hunters, stout, healthy, unmarried men, accustomed to the woods, and capable of bearing bodily fatigue in a pretty considerable degree."[21]

On 11 November 1803, Lewis and Clark arrived at Fort Massac, located on the Illinois side of the Ohio River. "The post was garrisoned by Captain Daniel Bissell's company of infantry, on which Lewis was authorized to draw volunteers."[22] They would find two suitable soldier volunteers and, excluding the captains, the expedition's most valuable participant, civilian interpreter and guide George Drouillard. Drouillard would prove invaluable for the duration of the expedition. Whenever the captains scouted ahead of the main body, "Drewyer" normally accompanied them. His service was held in such high regard that at the conclusion of the expedition, Lewis sought to provide him an extra $5 a month in addition to his $25 a month salary, which was already double that of the corps' noncommissioned officers.[23] Lewis and Clark expected to be met at Fort Massac by six to eight soldiers from South West Point, Tennessee. When the men failed to arrive, Drouillard was dispatched to locate them.

After turning north at the junction of the Ohio and Mississippi Rivers, the party rowed, poled, and heaved, against the current for the first time, en route to the expedition's next destination. They arrived at Fort Kaskaskia on 28 November. The fort was also located on the Illinois shore and was the home to "Captain Russell Bissell's infantry company, plus an artillery company commanded by Captain Amos Stoddard."[24] From Kaskaskia the Corps of Discovery would acquire more than a dozen men. Three weeks later Lewis wrote to Jefferson and reported that he had "'made a selection of a sufficient number of men from the troops of that place to complete my party.' He didn't say how many, but it probably was something more than a dozen, including the small-boat escort group plus men for the permanent party."[25] It is clear that Lewis and Clark had already decided to disregard their guidance to limit the endeavor to 10 to 12 men.

During the first week of December, Lewis sought clearance from Spanish officials headquartered at St. Louis for the expedition's passage up the Missouri. Months earlier respective heads of state had already signed the Louisiana Purchase, but at St. Louis the local military governor had yet to conduct the formal transfer ceremony, scheduled for the following spring. To avoid diplomatic wrangling and conceding that the 1803 travel season was largely over, Lewis decided to winter on the American side of the Mississippi, which would enable the corps to freely draw supplies and provisions from local Army units. An additional benefit of the meeting between Lewis and the local Spanish military governor of Louisiana, Carlos Dehault Delassus, was that Delassus recorded for future historians that Lewis' delegation now consisted of 25 men.[26]

It is difficult to determine an accurate head count between December 1803 and April 1804. The expedition's number fluctuated almost weekly as soldiers were welcomed and others dismissed.

> On December 22, Drouillard arrived at Clark's Camp Dubois with the eight lost soldiers from South West Point. They were a disappointing lot, except Corporal Richard Warfington. At some point two local experts on Missouri River travel, Pierre Cruzatte and Francois Labiche, agreed to help manage the keelboat. People kept drifting out. Four of the sad sacks from South West Point proved too sorry to keep. An individual name Leakens, recruited from somewhere, was discharged for theft.[27]

After locating a suitable spot across the river from St. Louis along the southern shore of the River Dubois, the party began construction of Camp Dubois. In a letter to Clark from Kaskaskia, Lewis noted that among the soldiers recruited from South West Point are "a blacksmith and House-joiner."[28] Both skills would prove invaluable to the operation.

Camp Dubois

During the winter, the captains continued to plan. Additional maps were acquired and created with the help of local traders. Discipline was expected and instilled by means of courts-martial and the subsequent meting out of harsh punishments. Additional supplies were purchased with the aid of local merchants, most notably the Chouteau brothers of St. Louis.[29] Improvements were made to the keelboat. Clark's field notes are littered with jottings regarding the preparedness of provisions and supplies. Lewis and Clark's winter of 1803-1804 shopping list (a sampling of the supplies obtained at St. Louis is located at Appendix H) included items such as: 19 small flags, 16 additional mosquito nets, 120 gallons of whiskey, 50 kegs of pork, 30 half-barrels of flour, 34 bushels of parched meal, two boxes of candles, 200 pounds of tallow, and dozens of kegs.[30] In addition to these supplies, the corps also acquired "a small forge, complete with bellows and fueled by charcoal, on which they could work iron and other metals. Shields and Willard were the smiths. Besides repairing expedition equipment, they made tomahawk heads and other articles to trade to the Indians for food."[31] The mass of goods and provisions purchased confirms the fact that the expedition was well on its way to expanding to more than three times its authorized strength.

Expecting an encounter with the Teton Sioux the following summer, Clark designed and supervised defensive improvements to the keelboat. Clark calculated and recorded the lumber and hardware required to add storage lockers to the keelboat's cargo hold. On 24 February 1804, he recorded that "10 pair of hinges" were mounted to the locker tops with 200 nails sent by Lewis.[32] The lockers enabled bulky equipment and provisions to be securely stowed while improving the vessel's defensive capability against Indian attacks. The hinged locker tops were sturdy enough to be walked on when closed. When the keelboat was threatened, the locker tops could be raised to form a solid defensive barricade running the length of the vessel.[33]

Presumably at Clark's urging, a small cannon or "swivel gun" capable of firing a 1-pound ball was mounted to the vessel's bow. The cannon was probably "held upon the forks of a Y-shaped mounting . . . the lower projection of the Y-shaped support, or swivel, was placed in a hole bored in the gunwale" of the keelboat.[34] Also at Clark's urging, the expedition acquired two blunderbusses, which were also mounted on swivels toward the boat's stern.[35] Both the cannon and the blunderbusses were formidable area weapons when loaded with a number of lead balls, nails, or even rocks. It is likely Clark believed that by having the keelboat display these weapons, the Teton

Sioux would be inclined to avoid a fight, having already experienced these weapons employed by Spanish forces patrolling the Missouri.[36]

> As the Missouri Company in 1795 extended its trading activities into the upper Missouri country, where British traders already had a following among the natives, some of the Spaniards… advocated a patrol of the river, 'with one or two galliots of small tonnage, flat-bottomed, and armed with six two-pound cannons, some swivel guns and manned by twenty sailors,' to be provided by the government.[37]

As previously stated, this expedition's growth was due to Lewis and Clark's suspicion that natives would attack the party if it did not appear sufficiently menacing. Clark noted in his journal that the party's safety "will Depend on the probability of an opposition from roving Parties of Bad Indians which it is probable may be on the [river]."[38] He later crossed out the comment, but the fact remains that Clark was concerned about the unit's ability to survive a confrontation.

On 25 September 1804, Clark's anxiety regarding the Teton Sioux proved correct. For approximately five days the party was extorted and threatened by the tribe. An example of the week's journal entries is provided below:

> Three of their young men Seased the Cable of the Perogue, the Chiefs Soldr. Huged the mast, and the 2d Chief was verry insolent both in words & justures declareing I Should not go on, Stateing he had not recved presents Suffient from us, his justures were of Such a personal nature I felt my Self Compeled to Draw my Sword, at this motion Capt. Lewis ordered all under arms in the boat, those with me also Showed a Disposition to Defend themselves and me, the grand Chief then took hold of the roop & ordered the young warrers away, I felt my Self warm & Spoke in verry positive terms. Most of the warriers appeared to have ther Bows Strung and took out their arrows from ther quves.[39]

Sergeant Ordway noted that the swivel gun was loaded with 16 balls and that the blunderbusses were loaded with buckshot.[40] Clearly Clark was right to insist on the additional arms, men, and the improvements to the keelboat's defenses undertaken during the winter of 1803-1804.

Following the ceremony transferring Louisiana from France to the United States, after years of planning and preparation, and after triple checking the loading and distribution of their cargo:

> all our provisions goods and equipage on Board of a Boat of 22 oars, a large Perogue of 7 oares a Second Perogue of 6 oars, 2 Complete with Sails &c. &c. men Compe. with Powder Cartragies and 100 Balls each, all in health and readiness to Set out. Boats and every thing Complete, with the necessary Stores of provisions & such articles of merchendize as we thought ourselves autherised to precure-- tho' not as much as I think necssy for the multitud of lnds. tho which we must pass on our road across the Continent &. &.[41]

The expedition set off, commanded by Clark, on 14 May 1804. Lewis, who had attended the transfer ceremony, would catch up with the group on 20 May. "All those who kept journals—Lewis, Clark, Gass, Ordway, Floyd, and Whitehouse dutifully record that the total number was about forty-five men. They do not all agree on the number, but none exceeds forty-five."[42] There very well could have been several more.

They were organized into three groups. The permanent party, those designated to make the journey to the Pacific and back, manned the keelboat. The return party set off in the red pirogue and would accompany the permanent party as far as the Mandan Villages, returning to St. Louis in the keelboat when ordered. The third group consisted of French boatmen or engagés. These men would guide the expedition up the river against the current to the Mandan Villages. Several engagés would return to St. Louis with the return party; others would remain with the Mandans or embark on other trade missions.[43]

The men of the Corps of Discovery had been hand selected by Lewis and Clark. They had formed into a solid, disciplined unit during their winter at Camp Dubois. Each member had something to offer the cause. Among them were carpenters, blacksmiths, a gunsmith, a tailor, musicians, interpreters, navigators, hunters, journalists, and above all, men that had bonded in the way only soldiers going into harm's way can comprehend. All were committed to their quest; all had unquestionable faith in their captains.

Notes

1. Gary E. Moulton, ed., *The Definitive Journals of Lewis and Clark*, 11 vols. (Lincoln: University of Nebraska Press, 2002-2003), 2:65.

2. Richard C. Boss, "Keelboat, Pirogue, and Canoe: Vessels Used by the Lewis and Clark Corps of Discovery," *Nautical Research Journal* (June 1999), 77.

3. Ibid.

4. Moulton, 4:108.

4. Boss, 79-80.

5. Ibid.

6. Moulton, 2:75.

7. Boss, 80.

8. Ibid.

9. Ibid., 81.

10. Ibid.

11. Donald Jackson, ed., *Letters of the Lewis and Clark Expedition, with Related Documents*: *1783-1854*, 2 vols., 2nd ed (Urbana: University of Illinois Press, 1978), 1:102-103.

12. Jackson, 1:103.

13. Ibid., 116.

14. Moulton, 2:66. Arlen J. Large, "Additions to the Party: How the Expedition Grew and Grew," *We Proceeded On* (February 1990), 6.

15. Large, 6.

16. Ibid.

17. Francis B. Heitman, *Historical Register and Dictionary of the United States Army, From its Organization, September 29, 1789, to March 2, 1903* (Urbana: University of Illinois Press, 1965), 2:568-69.

18. Jackson, 1:179.

19. Moulton, 2:513.

20. Jackson, 1:58.

21. Large, 7.

22. Jackson, 1:369.

23. Large, 7.

24. Ibid.

25. Jackson, 1:142-43.

26. Large, 7.

27. Jackson, 1:144.

28. William Foley, "The Lewis and Clark Expedition's Silent Partners: The Chouteau Brothers of St. Louis," *Missouri Historical Review* (Fall 1983), 136.

29. Moulton, 2:200, 2: 217-18.

30. Ibid., 3:262.

31. Boss, 72.

32. Ibid.

33. Carl P. Russell, *Guns On The Early Frontiers: A History of Firearms From Colonial Times Through The Years of the Western Fur Trade* (Lincoln: University of Nebraska Press, 1957), 252.

34. Jackson, 1:175.

35. Russell, 255.

36. Ibid.

37. Large, 7.

38. Moulton, 3:112.

39. Ibid., 9:68.

40. Ibid., 2:214-15.

41. Charles G. Clarke, *The Men of the Lewis and Clark Expedition: A Biographical Roster of the Fifty-One Members and a Composite Diary of Their Activities from All Known Sources* (Lincoln: University of Nebraska Press, 2002), 22-23.

42. Moulton, 3:227.

Chapter 6

Conclusion

Having invested 10 years pondering the possibilities, Captain Meriwether Lewis was perhaps the most qualified officer on the planet to develop the expedition's logistics support plan. His close relationship with President Jefferson enabled the pair to craft a politically acceptable and militarily plausible plan. Their initial cost estimate was purposely low to avoid congressional objections, just as the Louisiana Purchase was arguably beyond Jefferson's constitutional authority. It was apparently best to rapidly close the deal and then ask for Congress's forgiveness. It was with this mind-set the president achieved his goal of westward exploration. Once Congress authorized the expedition's initial funding ($2,500), Jefferson was confident that if the endeavor was successful, additional monies would be allocated without objection (the total price tag exceeded $39,000).[1] Likewise, if unsuccessful, cost overruns would be forgiven because of the expedition's politically shrewd secondary mission of "improving" the religion of the natives.

Jefferson provided Lewis with a letter of credit implying that it be used upon arrival at the Pacific to secure provisions, clothes, and passage for at least a few expedition members and scientific data. For reasons already stated, Jefferson likely verbally authorized his captain to purchase goods and services as required to accomplish his mission. Once distant from Washington, Lewis and Clark freely exceeded the personnel limitations specified by the authorization received from Congress and as communicated by the secretary of war.

Soon after arriving in the vicinity of St. Louis, the expedition's authorized strength had already doubled. Warnings from local traders supported Clark's misgivings about traversing Teton Sioux lands with a small party. By spring 1804 the party consisted of nearly 50 men. The larger party required the purchase of additional equipment and provisions from St. Louis merchants. Lewis and Clark freely hired interpreters, guides, and boatmen to facilitate their task. As the expedition's primary logistics planner, Lewis' foresight requires further examination.

Four themes regarding Lewis' logistics planning merit further discussion, namely the concept of innovation, the employment of civilian contractors, the anticipation of support from native tribes (host nation support), and difficulty in securing adequate transportation. Only the lack of transportation produced significant shortfalls during the operation.

Innovation

While Lewis' iron canoe ultimately failed, it exemplifies the spirit of innovation he brought to the enterprise. The inspiration for the canoe was probably native canoes made of stretched hides that he had observed on the frontier. He sought to improve on what he had seen by making his canoe collapsible and portable. Once the craft was covered with animal skins, only one easily obtainable item, pine tar, was required to make it watertight. The variety of pine tar available at Harper's Ferry proved elusive in Montana. The lesson for the modern logistician is not to assume that a critical item, readily available at one location, will be available at another.

When Lewis went to Harper's Ferry looking for 15 rifles, he was not seeking to create a new rifle type, nor would it be logical to do so. What he sought was 15 rifles with spare firing mechanisms. The concept of creating interchangeable parts was probably only acceptable to the artisans of the Harper's Ferry Armory in light of the unique mission at hand. The armory's craftsmen subscribed to the time-honored tradition that each weapon produced was a work of art. Acceptance of mass production techniques, with their associated reliance on interchangeable parts, would be accepted gradually. When Lewis headed west he possessed 15, decade-old contract rifles whose barrels had been shortened. One gunsmith would prove capable of keeping the expedition's weapons operational.

Knowing that he and his soldiers would be operating in a persistently damp environment and that the bulk containers provided by powder manufacturers were convenient but lacked the durability required for a lengthy operation, Lewis designed the expedition's most important innovation. The powder canisters were constructed in Philadelphia from 8 pounds of lead, had narrow corked mouths to seal out moisture, and were intended to refill the powder horns carried by soldiers. When empty, the containers would be melted and formed into balls. They performed magnificently. Expedition members never lacked an ample supply of dry powder or ball.

The revolutionary nature of the numbered storage bags Lewis had manufactured in Philadelphia is not immediately apparent. Without a doubt the articles were designed to overcome a problem exasperating logisticians even now. At issue is the ability to locate important items of equipment without searching through an entire load of cargo. The contemporary term applied to the concept is In Transit Visibility (ITV). Modern logisticians must be able to track supplies and equipment from their points of origin to their final destinations, often a distance of thousands of miles. Specialized tags and labels, able to communicate with various electronic devices, are applied to important items to locate them in the mountain of supplies at a port or storage location. During Operation *Desert Storm*, literally hundreds of containers arrived at ports with no means of determining their contents without opening them and inventorying their contents. To avoid the frustration of searching for a single tool in a mountain of equipment, Lewis had the foresight to number each of his storage bags, noting its contents before the party's departure from Camp Dubois.

Host Nation Support

Understanding that the expedition's success ultimately depended on establishing and maintaining friendly relations with the Indians encountered along the route, Lewis obtained a large supply of trade goods in Philadelphia and continued to augment the party's supply while wintering at Camp Dubois. Early in his planning he recognized that trade goods could, in addition to furthering purely diplomatic aims, be used to reduce shortfalls. The party freely dispensed trade goods along the route to obtain provisions, equipment, and services. The single most important transaction was with the Shoshone when the captains acquired 40 urgently needed horses to cross the fantastically underestimated Rocky Mountains. The services of several native guides also proved crucial to the expedition's success. Most notably, a native guide enabled the corps to locate a navigable route through the Rockies. While the corps members did run short on trade goods during their return trip, they used their ingenuity to transform remaining items and nonessential equipment into desirable trade objects. The host nation support provided by native tribes proved indispensable, often providing support at the expedition's most vulnerable moments. Recent military operations in Afghanistan have validated the essential nature of host nation support when attempting to conduct operations with a limited number of soldier-linguists and experienced guides.

Contractor Support

Modern military operations rely heavily on support from civilian contractors. This phenomenon is not new. Contractors contributed significantly to America's early military operations. There has been much hand wringing of late regarding the United States military's reliance on contractor support. Most critics of civilian contractors would never imagine that the Lewis and Clark Expedition relied heavily on contractor support. Lewis anticipated contractor support early in his planning. His initial estimate of expenses provided to Jefferson included a sum dedicated to hiring contractors.[2] Months later Jefferson's formal instructions for the expedition's conduct included the authority for Lewis to hire contractors. However, Jefferson anticipated the majority of Lewis' contracting support to occur upon his arrival at the Pacific.[3]

Lewis contracted wagon support, the construction of a keelboat, the services of a river pilot, and a team of oxen to pull the boat over a particularly shallow section of the Ohio. He also contracted for the services of two interpreters to accompany the expedition to the Pacific and back, as well as French boatmen to accompany the expedition to the Mandan Villages, and several native guides along the expedition route. One of these interpreters, George Drouillard, commonly referred to as "Drewyer" in expedition journals, was probably (excluding the captains) the party's most indispensable member. He was consistently with the captains during harrowing experiences and bagged the majority of game, often after periods of significant hardship. In the final analysis, Lewis contracted for goods and services far in excess of the $2,500 authorized by Congress. Lewis and Clark's experiences with contractors ranged the entire spectrum. In the end, Lewis' utter frustration with his drunken Pittsburgh boat contractor was probably offset by the extraordinary contributions of interpreter and hunter George Drouillard. It is likely that future generations of Americans will look at operations conducted in Afghanistan and Iraq and not adequately appreciate the integral role played by contractors.

Transportation

The Lewis and Clark Expedition was primarily a transportation exercise. As has been demonstrated, the endeavor was adequately provisioned and equipped. The operation's serious shortfalls regarded transportation. Of the 11 logistics functions recognized by the US Army, responsive transportation remains the most difficult to achieve. The Army regularly succeeds in achieving its operational objectives, but associated transportation timelines routinely exceed transportation estimates.

The captains failed to complete their mission within the two summers specified by the president. A month was squandered supervising the fabrication of Lewis' canoe at Harper's Ferry. An additional two months were lost waiting for the keelboat to be completed. These delays, together with the low water level of the Ohio River in September 1803, forced the expedition to spend the winter of 1803-1804 near St. Louis. After a grueling month-long portage of the Great Falls without the aid of horses, the party was again delayed when the iron canoe foundered. Lewis and Clark failed to anticipate the need for horses to assist their portage of the Great Falls. Assuming that these transportation shortfalls could have been avoided, the corps would have been poised to cross the Rockies in the spring rather than the fall of 1805. It is likely that a spring crossing would have enabled the expedition to arrive at the Pacific and return to St. Louis by December 1805, meeting Jefferson's intent of a two-summer mission.

In the end, it is likely that Jefferson considered Lewis and Clark's overdue return to be irrelevant and his two-season timeline the result of his personal impatience. The transportation challenges encountered by Lewis and Clark, although ultimately overcome with great success, illustrate that the most conspicuous "friction" encountered by military planners relates to the availability of adequate transportation assets. As with most challenges faced by the captains, transportation shortfalls were overcome by a combination of wit and tenacity.

Endings

Without a doubt the expedition was a success. Diplomatic and trade relationships were established with the Mandan, Shoshone, and Nez Perce tribes. Lewis provided Jefferson with scores of botanical and zoological discoveries. Clark used his notes to create accurate maps of the west.

Many of the logistics issues that confronted Lewis and Clark are very similar to questions that challenge today's logistics planners. Lewis and Clark's successful conduct of an incredibly complex and physically demanding operation has provided new insight as to how a logistician should prepare to venture into unknown territory. Groundbreaking missions require innovative methods to avoid logistics shortfalls. The movement of men and supplies over great distances has historically been the most challenging aspect of logistics planning and execution. Either by force or by voluntary agreement, host nation support is essential to most military operations. By far the most important factor influencing the outcome of a military operation is the personnel available to execute it. Lewis and Clark had the ability to observe potential expedition members, then handpick those deemed to have the skills and temperament for the task at hand.

Several historians have compared Lewis and Clark's mission to that of the Apollo 11, America's manned flight to the moon. The argument goes that Lewis and Clark traveled into the unknown, abandoning all communications with their government, while astronauts traveling to the moon remained in almost constant contact with ground controllers. Altitude and speed combine to provide dangers not easily overcome by communication alone. While some parallels exist, the analogy falls short when considering the remarkable contributions made by native Americans. Lewis and Clark had time, speed, and altitude on their side. Even when deep into lands previously unknown to men of European decent, expedition members could rely on their wits, an adaptable support plan, an ample supply of tools and arms, and the plentiful raw materials of our great nation to succeed.

Notes

1. Donald Jackson, ed., *Letters of the Lewis and Clark Expedition, with Related Documents: 1783-1854*, 2 vols., 2nd ed (Urbana: University of Illinois Press, 1978), 1:431.

2. Jackson, 1:9.

3. Ibid., 65.

Appendix A

Jefferson's Instructions to Lewis

To Meriwether Lewis, esquire, Captain of the 1st regiment of infantry of the United States of America.

Your situation as Secretary of the President of the United States has made you acquainted with the objects of my confidential message of Jan. 18, 1803, to the legislature. You have seen the act they passed, which, tho' expressed in general terms, was meant to sanction those objects, and you are appointed to carry them into execution.

Instruments for ascertaining by celestial observations the geography of the country thro' which you will pass, have been already provided. Light articles for barter, & presents among the Indians, arms for your attendants, say for from 10 to 12 men, boats, tents, & other travelling apparatus, with ammunition, medicine, surgical instruments & provisions you will have prepared with such aids as the Secretary at War can yield in his department; & from him also you will receive authority to engage among our troops, by voluntary agreement, the number of attendants above mentioned, over whom you, as their commanding officer, are invested with all the powers the laws give in such a case.

As your movements while within the limits of the U.S. will be better directed by occasional communications, adapted to circumstances as they arise, they will not be noticed here. What follows will respect your proceedings after your departure from the U.S.

Your mission has been communicated to the Ministers here from France, Spain, & Great Britain, and through them to their governments: and such assurances given them as to it's objects as we trust will satisfy them. The country of Louisiana having been ceded by Spain to France, the passport you have from the Minister of France, the representative of the present sovereign of the country, will be a protection with all its subjects: and that from the Minister of England will entitle you to the friendly aid of any traders of that allegiance with whom you may happen to meet.

The object of your mission is to explore the Missouri river, & such principal stream of it, as, by it's course & communication with the water of the Pacific ocean may offer the most direct & practicable water communication across this continent, for the purposes of commerce.

Beginning at the mouth of the Missouri, you will take observations of latitude and longitude at all remarkable points on the river, & especially at the mouths of rivers, at rapids, at islands & other places & objects distinguished by such natural marks & characters of a durable kind, as that they may with certainty be recognized hereafter. The courses of the river between these points of observation may be supplied by the compass, the log-line & by time, corrected by the observations themselves. The variations of the compass too, in different places should be noticed.

The interesting points of the portage between the heads of the Missouri & the water offering the best communication with the Pacific ocean should be fixed by observation, & the course of that water to the ocean, in the same manner as that of the Missouri.

Your observations are to be taken with great pains & accuracy to be entered distinctly, & intelligibly for others as well as yourself, to comprehend all the elements necessary, with the aid of the usual tables to fix the latitude & longitude of the places at which they were taken, & are to be rendered to the war office, for the purpose of having the calculations made concurrently by proper persons within the U.S. Several copies of these as well as of your other notes, should be made at leisure times, & put into the care of the most trustworthy of your attendants, to guard by multiplying them against the accidental losses to which they will be exposed. A further guard would be that one of these copies be written on the paper of the birch, as less liable to injury from damp than common paper.

The commerce which may be carried on with the people inhabiting the line you will pursue, renders a knolege of these people important. You will therefore endeavor to make yourself acquainted, as far as a diligent pursuit of your journey shall admit, with the names of the nations & their numbers;

> the extent & limits of their possessions;
> their relations with other tribes or nations;
> their language, traditions, monuments;
> their ordinary occupations in agriculture, fishing, hunting, war, arts, & the
> implements for these;
> their food, clothing, & domestic accommodations;
> the diseases prevalent among them, & the remedies they use;
> moral and physical circumstance which distinguish them

from the tribes they know; peculiarities in their laws, customs & dispositions; and articles of commerce they may need or furnish, & to what extent.

And considering the interest which every nation has in extending & strengthening the authority of reason & justice among the people around them, it will be useful to acquire what knolege you can of the state of morality, religion & information among them, as it may better enable those who endeavor to civilize & instruct them, to adapt their measures to the existing notions & practises of those on whom they are to operate.

Other objects worthy of notice will be
the soil & face of the country, it's growth & vegetable productions, especially
those not of the U.S.
the animals of the country generally, & especially those not known in the U.S.
the remains & accounts of any which may be deemed rare or extinct;
the mineral productions of every kind; but more particularly metals, limestone,
pit coal & saltpetre; salines & mineral waters, noting the temperature of the last
& such circumstances as may indicate their character;
volcanic appearances;
climate as characterized by the thermometer, by the proportion of rainy, cloudy
& clear days, by lightening, hail, snow, ice, by the access & recess of frost, by
the winds, prevailing at different seasons, the dates at which particular plants put forth lose their flowers, or leaf, times of appearance of particular birds, reptiles or insects.

Altho' your route will be along the channel of the Missouri, yet you will endeavor to inform yourself, by inquiry, of the character and extent of the country watered by its branches, & especially on it's Southern side. The North river or Rio Bravo which runs into the gulph of Mexico, and the North river, or Rio colorado which runs into the gulph of California, are understood to be the principal streams heading opposite to the waters of the Missouri, and running Southwardly. Whether the dividing grounds between the Missouri & them are mountains or flatlands, what are their distance from the Missouri, the character of the intermediate country, &

the people inhabiting it, are worthy of particular enquiry. The Northern waters of the Missouri are less to be enquired after, because they have been ascertained to a considerable degree, and are still in a course of ascertainment by English traders & travellers. But if you can learn anything certain of the most Northern source of the Mississippi, & of it's position relative to the lake of the woods, it will be interesting to us. Some account too of the path of the Canadian traders from the Mississippi, at the mouth of the Ouisconsin river, to where it strikes the Missouri, and of the soil and rivers in it's course, is desirable.

In all your intercourse with the natives treat them in the most friendly & conciliatory manner which their own conduct will admit; allay all jealousies as to the object of your journey, satisfy them of it's innocence, make them acquainted with the position, extent, character, peaceable & commercial dispositions of the U.S., of our wish to be neighborly, friendly & useful to them, & of our dispositions to a commercial intercourse with them; confer with them on the points most convenient as mutual emporiums, & the articles of most desirable interchange for them & us. If a few of their influential chiefs, within practicable distance, wish to visit us, arrange such a visit with them, and furnish them with authority to call on our officers, on their entering the U.S. to have them conveyed to this place at the public expense. If any of them should wish to have some of their young people brought up with us, & taught such arts as may be useful to them, we will receive, instruct & take care of them. Such a mission, whether of influential chiefs, or of young people, would give some security to your own party. Carry with you some matter of the kine pox, inform those of them with whom you may be, of it's efficacy as a preservative from the small pox; and instruct & encourage them in the use of it. This may be especially done wherever you may winter.

As it is impossible for us to foresee in what manner you will be received by those people, whether with hospitality or hostility, so is it impossible to prescribe the exact degree of perseverance with which you are to pursue your journey. We value too much the lives of citizens to offer them to probably destruction. Your numbers will be sufficient to secure you against the unauthorised opposition of individuals, or of small parties: but if a superior force, authorised or not authorised, by a nation, should be arrayed against your further passage, & inflexibly determined to arrest it, you must decline it's further pursuit, and return. In the loss of yourselves, we should lose also the information you will have acquired. By returning safely with that, you may enable us to renew the essay with better calculated means.

To your own discretion therefore must be left the degree of danger you may risk, & the point at which you should decline, only saying we wish you to err on the side of your safety, & to bring back your party safe, even if it be with less information.

As far up the Missouri as the white settlements extend, an intercourse will probably be found to exist between them and the Spanish posts at St. Louis, opposite Cahokia, or Ste. Genevieve opposite Kaskaskia. From still farther up the river, the traders may furnish a conveyance for letters. Beyond that you may perhaps be able to engage Indians to bring letters for the government to Cahokia or Kaskaskia, on promising that they shall there receive such special compensation as you shall have stipulated with them. Avail yourself of these means to communicate to us, at seasonable intervals, a copy of your journal, notes & observations of every kind, putting into cypher whatever might do injury if betrayed.

Should you reach the Pacific ocean, inform yourself of the circumstances which may decide whether the furs of those parts may not be collected as advantageously at the head of the Missouri (convenient as is supposed to the waters of the Colorado & Oregon or Columbia) as at Nootka sound or any other point of that coast; & that trade be consequently conducted through the Missouri & U.S. more beneficially than by the circumnavigation now practised.

On your arrival on that coast, endeavor to learn if there be any port within your reach frequented by the sea-vessels of any nation, and to send two of your trusty people back by sea, in such way as shall appear practicable, with a copy of your notes. And should you be of opinion that the return of your party by the way they went will be eminently dangerous, then ship the whole, & return by sea by way of Cape Horn or the Cape of Good Hope, as you shall be able. As you will be without money, clothes or provisions, you must endeavor to use the credit of the U.S. to obtain them; for which purpose open letters of credit shall be furnished you authorizing you to draw on the Executive of the U.S. or any of its officers in any part of the world, in which draughts can be disposed of, and to apply with our recommendations to the consuls, agents, merchants or citizens of any nation with which we have intercourse, assuring them in our name that any aids they may furnish you shall be honorably repaid, and on demand. Our consuls Thomas Howes at Batavia in Java, William Buchanan of the Isles of France and Bourbon, & John Elmslie at the Cape of Good Hope will be able to supply your necessities by draughts on us.

Should you find it safe to return by the way you go, after sending two of your party round by sea, or with your whole party, if no conveyance by sea can be found, do so; making such observations on your return as may serve to supply, correct or confirm those made on your outward journey.

In reentering the U.S. and reaching a place of safety, discharge any of your attendants who may desire & deserve it: procuring for them immediate paiment of all arrears of pay & cloathing which may have incurred since their departure and assure them that they shall be recommended to the liberality of the legislature for the grant of a souldier's portion of land each, as proposed in my message to Congress: & repair yourself with your papers to the seat of government.

To provide, on the accident of your death, against anarchy, dispersion & the consequent danger to your party, and total failure of the enterprise, you are hereby authorised, by any instrument signed & written in your own hand, to name the person among them who shall succeed to the command on your decease, & by like instruments to change the nomination from time to time, as further experience of the characters accompanying you shall point out superior fitness: and all the powers & authorities given to yourself are, in the event of your death, transferred to & vested in the successor so named, with further power to him, & his successors in like manner to name each his successor, who, on the death of his predecessor shall be invested with all the powers & authorities given to yourself.

Given under my hand at the city of Washington, this 20th. day of June 1803.

Th: J. Pr. U.S. of A.[1]

Notes

1. Donald Jackson, ed., *Letters of the Lewis and Clark Expedition, with Related Documents: 1783-1854*, 2 vols., 2nd ed (Urbana: University of Illinois Press, 1978), 1:61-66.

Appendix B

Lewis' List of Requirements

	Mathematical Instruments
1	Hadley's Quadrant
1	Mariner's Compas & 2 pole chain
1	Sett of plotting instruments
3	Thermometers
1	Cheap portable Microscope
1	Pocket Compass
1	brass Scale one foot in length
6	Magnetic needles in small straight silver or brass cases opening on the side with hinges.
1	Instrument for measuring made of tape with feet & inches mark'd on it
2	Hydrometers
1	Theodolite
1	Sett of planespheres
2	Artificial Horizons
1	Patent log
6	papers of Ink powder
4	Metal Pens brass or silver
1	Set of Small Slates & pencils
2	Creyons
	Sealing wax one bundle
1	Miller's edition of Lineus in 2 Vol:
	Books
	Maps
	Charts
	Blank Vocabularies
	Writing paper
1	Pair large brass money scales with two setts of weights

	Arms & Accoutrements
15	Rifle
15	Powder Horns & pouches complete
15	Pairs of Bullet Moulds
15	do. Of Wipers or Gun worms
15	Ball Screws
24	Pipe Tomahawks
24	large knives
	Extra parts of Locks & tools for repairing arms
15	Gun Slings
500	best Flints
200	Lbs. Best rifle powder
400	lbs. Lead

	Ammunition
200	Lbs. Best rifle powder
400	lbs. Lead

	Clothing
15	3 pt. Blankets
15	Watch Coats with Hoods & belts
15	Woolen Overalls
15	Rifle Frocks *of waterproof Cloth if possible* [emphasis in original]
30	Pairs of Socks or half Stockings
20	Fatigue Frocks or hinting shirts
30	Shirts of Strong linnen
30	yds. Common flannel.

	Camp Equipage
6	Copper kettles (1 of 5 Gallons, 1 of 3, 2 of 2, & 2 of 1)
35	falling Axes
4	Drawing Knives, short & strong
2	Augers of the patent kind
1	Small permanent Vice
1	Hand Vice
36	Gimblets assorted
24	Files do.
12	Chisels do.
10	Nails do.
2	Steel plate hand saws
2	Vials of Phosforus
1	do. Of Phosforus made of allum & sugar
4	Groce fishing Hooks assorted
12	Bunches of Drum Line
2	Foot Adzes
12	Bunches of Small cord
2	Pick Axes
3	Coils of rope
2	Spades
12	Bunches Small fishing line assorted
1	lb. Turkey or Oil Stone
1	Iron Mill for Grinding Corn
20	yds. Oil linnen for wrapping & securing Articles
10	yds do. do. Of thicker quality for covering and lining boxes. &c
40	yds Do. Do. To form two half faced Tents or Shelters
4	Tin blowing Trumpets
2	hand or spiral spring Steelyards
20	yds Strong Oznaburgs
24	Iron Spoons
24	Pint Tin Cups (without handles)
30	Steels for striking or making fire
100	Flints for do. do. do.
2	Frows
6	Saddlers large Needles
6	Do. Large Awls
	Muscatoe Curtains
2	patent chamber lamps & wicks
15	Oil Cloth Bags for securing provision
1	Sea Grass Hammock

Camp Equipage [Continued]	
30	Sheep skins taken off the Animal as perfectly whole as possible, without being split on the belly as usual and dress'd only with lime to free them from the wool; or otherwise about the same quantity of Oil Cloth bags well painted
	Raw hide for pack strings
	Dress'd letter for Hoppus-Straps
	Other packing

Provisions and Means of Subsistence	
150	lbs. Portable Soup.
3	bushels of Allum or Rock Salt
	Spicies assorted
6	Kegs of 5 Gallons each making 30 Gallons of rectified spirits such as is used for the Indian trade
6	Kegs bound with iron Hoops

	Indian Presents
5	lbs. White Wampum
5	lbs. White Glass Beads mostly small
20	lbs. Red Do. Do. Assorted
5	lbs. Yellow or Orange Do. Do. Assorted
30	Calico Shirts
12	Pieces of East India muslin Hanckerchiefs striped or check'd with brilliant Colours.
12	Red Silk Hanckerchiefs
144	Small cheap looking Glasses
100	Burning Glasses
4	Vials of Phosforus
288	Steels for striking fire
144	Small cheap Scizors
20	Pair large Do.
12	Groces Needles Assorted No. 1 to 8 Common points
12	Groces Do. Assorted with points for sewing leather
288	Common brass thimbles - part W. office
10	lbs. Sewing Thread assorted
24	Hanks Sewing Silk
8	lbs. Red Lead
2	lbs. Vermillion - at War Office
288	Knives Small such as are generally used for the Indian trade, with fix'd blades & handles inlaid with brass
36	Large knives
36	Pipe Tomahawks - *at H. Ferry* [emphasis in original]
12	lbs. Brass wire Assorted
12	lbs. Iron do. Do. generally large
6	Belts of narrow Ribbons colours assorted
50	lbs. Spun Tobacco.
20	Small falling axes *to be obtained in Tennessee*
40	fish Griggs such as the Indians use with a single barbed point - *at Harper's ferry* [emphasis in original]
3	Groce fishing Hooks assorted
3	Groce Mockerson awls assorted
50	lbs. Powder secured in a Keg covered with oil Cloth
24	Belts of Worsted feiret or Gartering Colours brilliant and Assorted
15	Sheets of Copper Cut into strips of an inch in width & a foot long
20	Sheets of Tin
12	lbs. Strips of Sheet iron 1 In. wide 1 foot long
1	Pc. Red Cloth second quality
1	Nest of 8 or 9 small copper kettles
100	Block-tin rings cheap kind ornamented with Colour'd Glass or Mock-Stone
2	Groces of brass Curtain Rings & sufficently large for the Finger
1	Groce Cast Iron Combs
18	Cheap brass Combs
24	Blankets.

Indian Presents [Continued]	
12	Arm Bands Silver at War Office
12	Wrist do. do. Do.
36	Ear Trinkets Do. Part do.
6	Groces Drops of Do. Part Do.
4	doz Rings for Fingers of do.
4	Groces Broaches of do.
12	Small Medals do.

Means of Transportation	
1	Keeled Boat light strong at least 60 feet in length her burthen equal to 8 Tons
1	Iron frame of Canoe 40 feet long
1	Large Wooden Canoe
12	Spikes for Setting-Poles
4	Boat Hooks & points Complete
2	Chains & Pad-Locks for confining the Boat & Canoes &c.

Medicine	
15	lbs. Best powder's Bark
10	lbs. Epsom or Glauber Salts
4	oz. Calomel
12	oz. Opium
1/2	oz. Tarter emetic
8	oz. Borax
4	oz. Powder'd Ipecacuana
8	oz. Powder Jalap
8	oz. Powdered Rhubarb
6	Best lancets
2	oz. White Vitriol
4	oz. Lacteaum Saturni
4	Pewter Penis syringes
1	Flour of Sulphur
3	Clyster pipes
4	oz. Turlingtons Balsam
2	lbs. Yellow Bascilicum
2	Sticks of Symple Diachylon
1	lb. Blistering Ointments
2	lbs. Nitre
2	lbs. Coperas

Materials for making up the Various Articles into portable Packs

30 Sheep skins taken off the Animal as perfectly whole as possible, without being split on the belly as usual and dress'd only with lime to free them from the wool; or otherwise about the same quantity of Oil Cloth bags well painted

Raw Hide for pack strings
Dress'd letter for Hoppus-Straps
Other packing

1. Blue beads. This is a coarse cheap bead imported from China, & costing in England 13 d. the lbs. in strands. It is far more valued than the white beads of the same manufacture and answers all the purposes of money, being counted by the fathom.

2. Common brass buttons more valued than any thing except beads.

3. Knives, with fixed wooden handles stained red, usually called red handled knives & such as are used by the N.W. Co. in their Indian trade.

4. Battle axes, and Tomahawks.

5. Saddlers seat awls, which answer for moccasin awls

6. Glove[r]'s Needles.

7. Cast Iron combs.

8. Nests of camp kettles; brass is much preferr'd to Iron, tho both are very useful to the Indians size from 1 to 4 gallons.[1]

---

1. Donald Jackson, ed., *Letters of the Lewis and Clark Expedition, with Related Documents: 1783-1854* (Urbana: University of Illinois Press, 1978), 1:69-74.

Appendix C
Items Obtained in Philadelphia

			Indian Presents	
			Wt.	
12	Pipe Tomahawks		8 3/4	18 ..
6 1/2	Strips Sheet Iron		6 1/2	1 62
1	Ps. Red flannel 47 1/2 yds		12 3/4	14 94
11	Ps. Hanckercheifs assd.		13 lb	59 83
1	doz. Ivory Combs		3 oz	3 33
1/2	Catty Inda. S. Silk		7 oz	3 75
21	lbs. Tread assd.		21 lb	23 17
1	Ps. Scarlet Cloth 22 yds		28 3/4	58 50
5 1/2	doz fancy 1 Floss	6 3/4		18 87
6	Gro. Binding	9 1/4	26 1/2	11 79
2	Cards Beads	1 3/4		3 80
4	doz. Butcher Knives	8 3/4		5 33
12	doz. Pocket Looking Glasses		12 1/2 lb	5 19
15	doz. Pewter do. do.		3 6/16	3 99
8	doz. Burning do.		11 1/4	12 00
2	doz. Nonesopretty		3 1/4	2 94
2	doz. Red strip'd tapes		1 1/2	2 80
72	ps. Strip'd silk ribbon		3 1/4	39 60
3	lbs. Beads		3 lb	2 01
6	Papers Small Bells		1 1/4	4 02
1	box with 100 larger do.		1 3/16	2 25
73	Bunches Beads assd.		20	41 ..
3 1/2	doz: Tinsel Bands assd.		9 oz	3 75
1	doz: Needle Cases		5 1/2 oz	30
2 3/4	doz. Lockets		3 oz	3 56
8 1/2	lbs. Red Beads		8 1/2	25 50
2	doz. Earings			1 ..
8	Brass Kettles a 4/ Per lb.		20 lbs.	10 67
12	lbs. Brass Strips			6 80
500	Broaches		1 1/2	62 07
72	Rings			6 00
2	Corn Mills		52 3/4	20 00
15	doz. Scissors		17 1/4	18 97
12	lbs. Brass Wire			7 80
14	lbs. Knitting Pins		14	3 89
4800	Needles assd.		2 1/4	9 73
2800	Fish Hooks assd.		6 1/8	8 ..
1	Gro. Iron Combs		8 1/2	2 80

	Indian Presents - Continued			
3	Gro. Curtain Rings		1 3/4	1 87
2	Gro. Thimbles assd.		2 1/2	3 21
11	doz. Knives		37	25 17
10	lbs. Brads		16	1 00
8	lbs. Red lead		8	89
2	lbs. Vermillion		2	3 34
130	Rolls of Tobacco (pigtail)		63	14 25
48	Callico Ruffled Shirts			71 04
15	Blankets (from P. Store)			
1	Trunk to pack sundry Ind. Prests.			3 50
8	Groce Seat or Mockasin Awls			15.67
				669.5
	From Public Store--vizt. 15 Blanket			

	Camp Equipage		
		Wt.	
4	Tin Horns	1 3/4	2 ..
2	" Lanthorns	1	2 ..
2	" Lamps.	1/2	50
32	" Cannisters of P. Soup	193	8 ..
1	" Box sqr. Of Small art	1 1/2	1 ..
3	doz Pint Tumblers	6 1/2	4 20
125	Large fishg Hooks		4 45
	Fishg Lines assorted	10 1/2	18 09
1	Stand of Fishg do. With hooks Complete		3 ..
1	Sportsmans Flaske		1 50
8	ps. Cat gut for Mosquito Curt.	11	15 50
6	Brass Kettles & Porterage 25 cts.	28	15 18
1	block tin Sauce pan	3/4	1 50
1	Corn Mill	20	9 ..
1	Set of Gold Scales & Wts.	1/4	2 33
1	Rule	1 oz	60
1	Sett Iron Weights	4	75
2	pr. Large Shears	3 1/2	1 86
4	doz Packg. Needles & large Awls	1 .	1 13
2	doz Table Spoons	3	1 87
4	drawing Knives	2 1/2	1 20
3	doz Gimblets	5 1/4 lbs	3 60
17	do. Files & Rasps & 1 Shoe float	5	2 31
1 1/4	doz. Small cord	8 1/2	1 79
2	Small Vices		1 67
2	pr. Plyers	10	97
1	Saw Sett		10
9	Chisels		1 77
2	Adzes	4	1 20
2	hand Saws	4 1/2	3 06
6	Augers 6	3 1/2	1 64
2	Hatchets		83
1	Wetstone	4 1/2	47
2	p. Pocket steel yards		47
	Pkg 12 lbs Castile Soap	2	1 68
			117 67

	Camp Equipage [Continued] - From Public Store.	
8	Receipt nooks	
48	ps. Tape	
6	Brass Inkstands	
6	Papers Ink Powder	
1	Common Tent	
1	lb. Sealing Wax	
100	Quils	
1	Packing Hogshead	

	Camp Equipage [Continued] - Bought by the Purveyor of Richd. Wevill	
8	Tents	
45	Bags	
10	yd. Country Linnen	Oiled
20	" Brown do.	

			Medicines &c				
15 lb.	Pulv. Cort. Peru	30		4 oz.	Laudanum		.50
1/2 lb.	" Jalap	.67		2 lb.	Ung. Basilic Flav., .50		1.00
1/2 lb.	" Rhei (Rhubarb)	1.00		1 lb.	" e lap Cailmin. .50		.50
4 oz	" Ipecacuan	1.25		1 lb.	" Epispastric		1.00
2 lb.	" Crem. Tart.	.67		1 lb.	" Mercuriale		1.25
2 oz	Gum Camphor	.40		1.	Emplast. Diach. S.		.50
1 lb.	" Assafoetic	1.00		1.	Set Pocket Insts. Small		9.50
1/2 lb.	" Opii Turk. Opt	2.50		1.	" Teeth " "		2.25
1/4 lb.	" Tragacanth	.37		1.	Clyster Syringe		2.75
6 lb.	Sal Glauber	.60		4.	Penis do.		1.00
2 lb.	" Nitri .33 1/2	.67		3.	Best Lancets		2.40
2 lb.	Copperas	.10		1.	Tourniquet		3.50
6 oz	Sacchar. Saturn. Opt.	.37		2oz	Patent Lint		.25
4 oz	Calomel	.75		50 doz.	Bilious Pills to Order of Dr. Rush		5.00
1 oz	Tartar Emetic	.10		6	Tin Canisters .25		1.50
4 oz	Vitriol Alb.	.12		3	8 oz. Gd. Stopd. Bottles		1.20
1/2 lb.	Columbo Rad.	1.00		5	4 oz. Tinctures do		1.85
1/4 lb.	Elix. Vitriol	.25		6	4 oz. Salt Mo.		2.22
1/4 lb.	Ess. Meth. Pip.	.50		1	Walnut Chest		4.50
1/4 lb.	Bals. Copaiboe	.37		1	Pine do.		1.20
1/4 lb.	" Traumat.	.50					$90.69
2 oz	Magnesia	.20					
1/4 lb.	Indian Ink	1.50					
2 oz	Gun Elastic	.37					
2 oz	Nutmegs	.75					
2 oz	Cloves	.31					
4 oz	Cinnamon	.20					
		$46.52					

Medicines &c [Recapitulation]		
1	Box	$90.69
1	do.	
2	lbs. Tea & Cannister W. 2 lbs.	3.80
		94.49

Provisions &c		
		Dolls. Cts
193	lbs. P. Soup	289 50
30	Galls. Spr. Of Wine in 6 Kegs	77 20
		366 70
		Dolls. Cts
45	Flannel Shirts	71 10
16	Coatees	246 63
		317 73
Provisions &c [Continued] - From Public Stores vizt.		
15	Blankets	
15	Watch Coats	
15	Ps. Blue wool. Overalls	
36	pairs Stockgs.	
20	Frocks	
30	Pr. Shirts	
20	Pr.Shoes	

Arms & Accoutrements & Ammn.			
		lbs	
1	Pair Pocket pistols (P. by L.)		10 ..
176	lb. Gun powder	176	155 75
52	leaden Cannisters for Gunpowr	420	26 33
15	Powder Horns & Pouches.		26 25
Arms & Accoutrements & Ammn. Continued - From Public Store			
15	Powder Horns & Pouches		
18	Tomahawks		
15	Scalpking Knives & Belts		
15	Gun Slings		
30	Brushes & Wires		
15	Cartouch Boxes		
15	painted Knapsacks		
500	Rifle Flints		
125	Musket do.		
50	lb. Best rifle Powder		
1	pr. Horsemans Pistols		
420	lbs. Sheet Lead		

Mathematical Instruments			
1	Spirit level		4 ..
1	Case platting Instruments		14 ..
1	Two pole chain		2 ..
1	Pocket Compas plated		5 ..
1	Brass Boat Compass		1 50
3	Brass Pocket Compasses		7 50
1	Magnet		1 ..
1	Hadleys Quadrant with Tangt Screw		22 ..
1	Metal Sextant		90 ..
	Microscope to index of d		7 ..
	Sett of Slates in a case		4 ..
4	oz of Talc		1 25
1	Surveying Compass with extra needles	(P by L)	23 50
1	Circular protractor & index	do.	8 ..
1	Six In. Pocket Telescope	do.	7 ..
1	Nautical Ephemeris [Book]	do.	1 50
1	Requisite Tables	do.	2 50
1	Kirwan's Mineralogy [Book]	do.	5 ..
1	Chronometer & Keys		250 75
1	Copy Bartons Bottony (pd. By C. L.) [Book]		6 ..
1	Kelleys Spherics [Book]	do.	3 ..
2	Nautical Ephemeris [Book]	do.	4 ..
	Log line reel & log ship		1 95
	Parrellel Glass for a Horison		1 ..

Source: Donald Jackson, ed., *Letters of the Lewis and Clark Expedition, with Related Documents: 1783-1854* (Urbana: University of Illinois Press, 1978), 1:79-99.

Appendix D

Rush's Rules of Health*

Dr. Rush to Capt. Lewis for preserving his health.
June 11. 1803.

1. When you feel the least indisposition, do not attempt to overcome it by labour or marching. Rest in a horizontal posture. Also fasting and diluting drinks for a day or two will generally prevent an attack of fever. To these preventatives of disease may be added a gentle sweat obtained by warm drinks, or gently opening the bowels by means of one, two or more of the purging pills.
2. Unusual costiveness is often a sign of approaching disease. When you feel it take one or more of the purging pills.
3. Want of appetite is likewise a sign of approaching indisposition. It should be obviated by the same remedy.
4. In difficult & laborious enterprises & marches, eating sparingly will enable you to bear them with less fatigue & less danger to your health.
5. Flannel should be worn constantly next to the skin, especially in wet weather.
6. The less spirit you use the better. After being wetted or much fatigued, or long exposed to the night air, it should be taken in an undiluted state. 3 tablespoonfuls taken in this way will be more useful in preventing sickness, than half a pint mixed with water.
7. Molasses or sugar & water with a few drops of the acid of vitriol will make a pleasant & wholesome drink with your meals.
8. After having had your feet much chilled, it will be useful to wash them with a little spirit.
9. Washing the feet every morning in cold water, will conduce very much to fortify them against the action of cold.
10. After long marches, or much fatigue from any cause, you will be more refreshed by lying down in a horizontal posture for two hours, than by resting a much longer time in any other position of the body.
11. Shoes made without heels, by affording equal action to all the muscles of the legs, will enable you to march with less fatigue, than shoes made in the ordinary way.

*David J. Peck, *Or Perish in the Attempt: Wilderness Medicine in the Lewis and Clark Expedition* (Helena, MT: Farcountry Press, 2002), 50.

Appendix E

Rush's Questions*

I. Physical History and Medicine

What are the acute diseases of the Indians? Is the bilious fever attended with a black vomit.

Is Goiture, apoplexy, palsy, Epilepsy, madness . . . ven. Disease known among them?

What is their state of life as to longevity?

At what age do the women begin and cease to menstruate?

At what age do they marry? How long do they suckle the Children?

What is the provision of their Childrn. After being weaned?

The state of the pulse as to frequency in the morning, at noon & at night-before & after eating? What is its state in childhood. Adult life, & old age? The number of strokes counted by the quarter of a minute by glass, and multiplied by four. Will give its frequency in a minute. What are their Remidies?

Are artificial discharges of blood ever used among them?

In what manner do they induce sweating?

Do they ever use voluntary fasting?

At what time do they rise-their Baths?

What is the diet-manner of cooking & times of eating among the Indians? How do they preserve their food?

II. Morals

1. What are their vices?
2. Is Suicide common among them?-ever from love?
3. Do they employ any substitute for ardent spirits to promote intoxication?
4. Is murder common among them, & do they punish it with death?

III. Religion

1. What Affinity between their religious Ceremonies & those of the Jews?
2. Do they Use animal Sacrifices in their worship?
3. What are the principal Objects of their worship?
4. How do they dispose of their dead, and with what Ceremonies do they inter them?

> May 17, 1803
> B. Rush

*Excerpted from Eldon G. Chuinard, *Only One Man Died: The Medical Aspects of the Lewis & Clark Expedition* (Fairfield, WA: Ye Galleon Press, 1998), 151-52.

Appendix F

Medicines of the Lewis and Clark Expedition*

*Excerpted from David J. Peck, *Or Perish in the Attempt: Wilderness Medicine in the Lewis and Clark Expedition* (Helena, MT: Farcountry Press, 2002), 321-24.

Pharmaceutical Terms

Analgesics. Drugs that produce pain relief.

Astringents. Drugs that harden or contract tissues.

Carminatives. Drugs that produce a feeling of comfort in the stomach and intestines and relieve the formation of gas.

Cathartic. Acts on the intestines to stimulate bowel movements.

Counterirritants. Drugs that act on the skin causing redness. They were believed to relieve inflammation in remote organs or tissues. By acting on the nerve endings in the skin they also relieve pain in remote organs.

Dermatitis. Inflammation of the skin.

Diaphoretics. Drugs that produce perspiration.

Diuretics. Drugs that increase the production of urine in the kidneys.

Emetics. Drugs that produce vomiting.

Emollients. Drugs that soften and protect the skin.

Lavage. The act of washing a tissue with some solution.

Purgatives. Drugs that stimulate bowel movements, same as cathartic.

Poultices. Drugs that were applied to the skin to relieve pain or to dilate blood vessels on the skin, functioning as a counterirritant.

Resins. Thick, sticky chemicals from the sap of various trees; many were dissolved in alcohol.

Stimulants. Drugs that stimulate the patient, causing an increased level of consciousness, activity.

Tinctures. Drugs mixed in an alcoholic solution.

Tonics. Drugs that were thought to increase vigor and health.

Lewis & Clark's Medicine Chest

Assafoetic. Ill smelling (similar to garlic) Indian spice, used as a carminative to lessen abdominal distention, abdominal cramping. No documented use during the expedition.

Balsam copaiba. An oily, resinous substance from the South American leguminous tree, genus *Copaifera*, containing benzoic or cinnamic acid. Probably used as a carminative, diuretic, or orally as a treatment for gonorrhea. It is possible that this was also used in solution to lavage the penile urethra with a penile syringe in treatment of gonorrhea. It can also be used to treat contact dermatitis.

Balsamum traumaticum. This substance contains benzoin (a thickened sap from the Peruvian tree *Styrax benzoini*), aloes, and balsam of tolu, from the plant *Myroxylon bal-samum* (a sticky reddish substance that dissolves in alcohol but not in water). Likely used to treat respiratory problems by increasing respiratory secretions, and in inflammations of the nose, throat, and bronchi.

Calamine ointment. Mixture of zinc oxide and ferric oxide, used as an ointment to reduce skin irritations.

Calomel. Mercurous chloride, used principally as a purgative. Increases bile duct secretion producing dark stools; also a diuretic; given orally, has an anti-syphilitic action; ingredient of Dr. Rush's Bilious Pills.

Cream of tartar. Derived from the juice of grapes and deposited in wine casks together with yeast, a purgative.

Dr. Rush's Bilious Pills. A potent combination of calomel and jalap. Used for many ills during the expedition. Lewis bought 50 dozen of them to take along.

Epispastric ointment. Used to produce blisters on the skin to act as a counterirritant, which was thought to withdraw fluid from deeper tissue into the blister, thus competing with tissue excitability elsewhere. The active substance is a cantharide, obtained from dried beetles found in various temperate climates, especially in Spain and Italy.

Glauber's salts. Sodium sulfate, a saline cathartic.

Gum camphor. When taken internally it is a stimulant and diaphoretic. Obtained from the camphor tree, *Cinnamomum camphora*, a large evergreen of the laurel family. Also used on skin diseases as a counterirritant, which causes mild skin irritation, a feeling of warmth, and analgesia for aches and pains.

Ipecacuan. From the roots of the Brazilian tree *Cephaelis ipecacuanaha*. A favorite of producing emesis, used sparingly on the expedition.

Jalap. A drastic cathartic obtained from the Mexican vine *Exogonium jalapa*. Among the ingredients of Dr. Rush's "Thunderclapper" pills.

Laudanum. Tincture of opium, about a 10 percent opium solution. First concocted in 1510.

Magnesia. A cathartic magnesium salt.

Mercury ointment. The mainstay of syphilis treatment. Applied directly to the lesion and other areas of the body. The patient was often treated until they showed signs of mercury poisoning such as excessive salivation or sore gums.

Nutmeg, cloves, and cinnamon. Used to flavor foul-tasting medicines as well as lessen the cramping action of cathartics.

Peruvian bark. The corps took more of this than any other medicine, 15 pounds in the powdered form. Obtained from the genus *Cinchona*, a tree of Peru; used as a tonic and in many concoctions for fever, snakebites, abdominal pain, and just about anything else. Contains quinine, which was effective against "ague" or malaria.

Rhubarb. A purgative, cathartic (powdered).

Sugar of lead. Lead acetate, used in eye washes. On the return trip, the captains traded medical services, especially this treatment, with Indians of the Columbia River drainage.

Tartar emetic. An antimony-potassium compound, with a sweet, metallic taste, which produces vomiting.

Tragacanth. A gummy exudate from the plant *Astragalum gummifor*, a non-greasy lubricant used in lotions, emollients.

Turkish opium. Obtained from immature capsules of the opium poppy, *Papaver somniferum*, used to relieve pain, and as a sedative to lessen nervous excitability. Mixed with alcohol to make laudanum.

White vitriol. Zinc sulfate, used with lead acetate in the captains' eyewash. The corps carried only 4 ounces.

Wine (30 gallons) and whiskey. Medicinal (of course!), following Dr. Rush's prescription. The expedition ran out of whiskey on the Fourth of July 1805.

Instruments and Other Supplies

Best lancets (3). Used to cut open a vein and get rid of blood.

Clyster syringe (1). A large syringe used to administer enemas.

"Emplast. Diach. S." Lead oleate, a plaster of lead probably used as a casting material, or to apply to the skin after it was spread with medication on muslin or leather.

Penis syringes (4). Likely to administer penile lavages of balsam of copaiba to treat gonorrhea. The journals do not mention the use of these items.

Pocket instruments. Likely small surgical instruments.

Teeth instruments. Dental instruments.

Tourniquet (1)

Patent lint. Used to pack wounds, especially Captain Lewis' gunshot in the buttocks.

Various canisters, tincture bottles, all stored in a walnut chest and a pine chest.

Appendix G

Roster of Personnel

			Joined the Expedition From:						
	Rank	Name	Kaskaskia	Massac	South West Point	St. Louis Region	Kentucky	Mandan	Remarks
1	Captain	Lewis, Meriwether							The president's former secretary.
2	Second Lieutenant	Clark, William					X		Participants believed he held a captain's commission.
3	Sergeant	Floyd, Charles					X		Maintained a journal. Died 20 August 1804.
4	Sergeant	Gass, Patrick	X						Promoted after Floyd's death. Skilled carpenter.
5	Sergeant	Ordway, John	X						Maintained a journal. Only sergeant from the regular army.
6	Sergeant	Pryor, Nathaniel					X		Married. No journal found.
7	Private	Bratton, William	X				X		Skilled hunter and blacksmith.
8	Private	Collins, John	X*						Court-martialed for stealing whiskey.
9	Private	Colter, John					X		Skilled hunter.
10	Private	Cruzatte, Pierre				X			Former French boatman. Half Omaha. One-eyed and nearsighted. Entertained with his fiddle.
11	Private	Field, Joseph					X		Crack shot. Skilled hunter. Reubin's brother.
12	Private	Field, Reubin					X		Crack shot. Skilled hunter. Joseph's brother.
13	Private	Frazer, Robert	X*						Transferred to permanent party after Reed's expulsion.
14	Private	Gibson, George					X		Skilled hunter. Played fiddle. Interpreter.
15	Private	Goodrich, Silas	X*				X	X	Possible resident of Missouri prior to expedition.
16	Private	Hall, Hugh			X				Court-martialed for stealing whiskey.
17	Private	Howard, Thomas P.			X				Court-martialed for scaling the wall of Fort Mandan.
18	Private	La Page, John Baptiste						X	
19	Private	Labiche, Francois	X						Former French boatman. Half French, half Omaha. Skilled boatman and Indian trader.
20	Private	McNeal, Hugh	Unknown						May have been in the Army prior to expedition.

	Rank	Name	Kaskaskia	Massac	South West Point	St. Louis Region	Kentucky	Mandan	Remarks
			Permanent Party (Cont.)						
			Joined the Expedition From:						
21	Private	Potts, John			X				German born.
22	Private	Shannon, George					X		Separated from the party for two weeks in the fall of 1804, almost starved.
23	Private	Shields, John							Skilled armorer.
24	Private	Thompson, John B.	Unknown						Possible experience as a surveyor.
25	Private	Weiser, Peter	X						
26	Private	Werner, William	Unknown						Convicted of being absent without leave at outset of expedition.
27	Private	Whitehouse, Joseph		X					Maintained a journal. Acted as tailor.
28	Private	Willard, Alexander	X						Skilled blacksmith. Court-martialed for sleeping on sentry duty at Camp Dubois. Received 100 lashes. Former member of Captain Stoddard's company.
29	Private	Windsor, Richard	X*						Skilled hunter.
30	Civilian	Charbonneau, Baptiste "Pomp"						X	Sacagawea and Toussaint's infant son.
31	Civilian	Charbonneau, Toussaint						X	Bumbling interpreter.
32	Civilian	Drouillard, George		X					Skilled hunter, interpreter and guide
33	Civilian	Sacagawea						X	Wife of Toussaint Charbonneau, Shoshone interpreter.
34	Civilian	York					X		Clark's slave. Companion and "servant" since boyhood.

100

	Rank	Name	Kaskaskia	Massac	South West Point	St. Louis Region	Kentucky	Mandan	Remarks
			Joined the Expedition From:						
1	Corporal	Warfington, Richard			X				Reliable. Charged with leading the return party.
2	Private	Boley, John	X						
3	Private	Dame, John	X						Former member of Captain Stoddard's company.
4	Private	Newman, John		X					Court-martialed, received 75 lashes and was expelled from the party.
5	Private	Reed, Moses B.	Unknown						Court-martialed for "mutinous expression," was expelled from the party.
6	Private	Robertson, John	X						Possibly demoted from corporal at Camp Dubois.
7	Private	Tuttle, Ebenezer	X						Former member of Captain Stoddard's company.
8	Private	White, Isaac	X						Former member of Captain Stoddard's company.

Return Party

		Engages						
		Joined the Expedition From:						
	Name	Kaskaskia	Massac	South West Point	St. Louis Region	Kentucky	Mandan	Remarks
1	Cann, E.				X			First mentioned 4 July 1804. Member of return party.
2	Caugee, Charles				X			First mentioned 4 July 1804. Return party
3	Collin, Joseph				X			Mentioned only on 26 May 1804 list. May have been discharged at Fort Mandan.
4	Deschamps, Jean Baptiste				X			Foreman of boatmen
5	Hebert, Charles				X			May have been discharged at Fort Mandan.
6	La Jeunesse, Jean Baptiste				X			Discharged at Fort Mandan.
7	La Liberte	Hired En Route						Quit the expedition.
8	Malboeuf, Etienne				X			Member of return party.
9	Pinaut, Peter				X			Mentioned only on May 26, 1804.
10	Primeau, Paul				X			Discharged at Fort Mandan.
11	Rivet, Francois				X			May have left the return party.
12	Roi, Peter				X			Discharged at Fort Mandan.

ˣ Generally believed to have joined the expedition from Fort Kaskaskia.

Source: Gary E. Moulton, ed., *The Definitive Journals of Lewis and Clark* (Lincoln: University of Nebraska Press, 2002), 2:509-29.

102

Appendix H

Supplies Obtained in St. Louis and Final Inventory

14 April 1804*	
Received of Major Runsey	14th apl.
14 flour Kegs	
19 Pork Kegs	
537 [lb?] Salt	
April 1804 - Received by Clark at Camp Dubois**	
200 Nails 6d or 8d to put on Hinges	
5 Bar: Corml	
2 Trumpits to be mended.	
2000 lbs Pork sent 5 barrels	
2000 " Flour do. 5 do. Of Contr. To be furnished	
sent 251/2 bushels of lyed com	
2 May 1804 - Sent by Lewis to Clark from St. Louis**	
19 small flaggs	
Sixteen Musquitoe nets	
"our shirts" [officer's shirts?]	
6 May 1804 - Sent by Lewis to Clark from St. Louis**	
200 lbs. of tallow	
50 lbs. of hog's lard	

14 May 1804 - Final Inventory	w [lbs]
14 Bags of Parch meal of 2 bus: each about	1200
9 do Common Do do do	800
11 do Corn Hulled do do	1000
30 half Barrels of flour	Gross 390
3 Bags of do	
7 do of Biscuit	Gross 650
4 Barrels do	
7 Barrels of Salt of 2 bus: each " (870) do	750
50 Kegs of Pork (gross 4500) do	gross 4500
2 Boxes of Candles 70 lb and about 50 lb (one of which has 50 lb of soap [)] do	170
1 Bag of Candle-wick do	8
1 do Coffee	50
1 do Beens & 1 of Pees	100
2 do Sugar do	112
1 Keg of Hogs Lard do	100
4 Barrels of Corn hulled (650) do	600
1 do of meal (170) do	150
Grees	600 lb
50 bushels meal	
24 do Natchies Corn Huled	
21 Bales of Indian goods	
Tools of every Description & &.	

*Source: Gary E. Moulton, *The Definitive Journals of Lewis and Clark* (Lincoln: University of Nebraska Press, 2002), 2:202, 2:217-18.

**Source: Donald Jackson, *Letters of the Lewis and Clark Expedition, with Related Documents: 1783-1854* (Urbana: University of Illinois Press, 1978), 1:175-77.

Appendix I
Cache Detail

Items Cached 9-12 June 1805 - Vicinity Marias River				
As Recorded In Lewis' Journal	As Recorded In Other Journals			Date Recovered
	Clark	Ordway	Whitehouse	
tin cannester of 4 lbs. Of powder and an adequate quantity of lead*	X			28 July 1806
an axe**				" "
1 Cannester of 6 lbs. Lead**	X			" "
one Keg of 20 lbs. [powder]		X	X	" "
an adequate proportion of lead	X	X	X	" "
2 best falling axes	X	X		" "
an auger	X	X	X	" "
1 set of plains	X	X	X	" "
some files	X			" "
Blacksmiths bellowses and hammers Stake tongs &c.	X	X	X	" "
1 Keg of flour	X	X	X	" "
2 Kegs of parched meal	X	X	X	Spoiled
1 Keg of Pork	2 Kegs Pork	1 Keg	1 Keg	28 July 1806
1 Keg of salt	X			" "
some chissels	X			" "
Coper's Howel	X			" "
some tin cups	X	X	X	" "
2 Musquets				Never Cached****
3 brown bear skins	X	X	X	28 July 1806
beaver skins	X	X	X	" "
horns of a bighorned animal	X	X		" "
a part of mens robes clothing and superfluous baggage of every description	X	X	X	" "
beaver traps***	X	X	X	Not Found
		dutch oven	X	No record
			corn hand mill	No record

* 10 June 1805-cache one
** 10 June 1805-cache two
*** Traps cached on 12 June. Traps intended to be placed in "large Cash" on 11 June 1805.
**** Blunderbusses actually cached at Lower Falls Camp.

Items Cached 26 June 1805 - Vicinity Lower Portage Camp				
As Recorded In Lewis' Journal	As Recorded In Other Journals			Date Recovered
	Clark	Ordway	Whitehouse	
2 Kegs of Pork	X			26 July 1806
1/2 a Keg of flour	X			" "
2 blunderbushes	X			" "
1/2 a keg of fixed ammunition	X			" "
some other small articles	X			" "
swivel and carrage				" "

Items Cached 9 July 1805 Vicinity Upper Portage Camp				
As Recorded In Lewis' Journal	As Recorded In Other Journals			Date Recovered
	Clark	Ordway	Whitehouse	
desk, books, my specimens of plants minerals &c. collected from fort Mandan to that place*	X			Items found water damaged 13 July 1806
Iron canoe	X	X	X	No record

Items Cached 20 August 1805 - Vicinity Camp Fortunate				
As Recorded In Lewis' Journal	As Recorded In Other Journals			Date Recovered
	Clark	Ordway	Whitehouse	
small assortment of medicines, together with the specemines of plants, minerals, seeds I have collected between this place and the falls of the Missouri		X*	X*	8 July 1806
Baggage		X	X	" "
Emplacement Not Recorded				
tobacco				8 July 1806

* Cache mentioned, contents not provided

Items Cached 6 October 1805 - Vicinity Canoe Camp				
As Recorded In Clark's Journal	As Recorded In Other Journals			Date Recovered
	Lewis*	Ordway	Whitehouse	
Saddles		X	X	"Half" of saddles salvaged 9 May 1806
Emplacement not recorded				
Powder and lead*				Recovered with saddles 9 May 1806

* Only spotty journal entries exist for Lewis between August 1805 and January 1806.

Items Cached 7 October 1805 - Clearwater River				
Recovery Recorded in Lewis' Journal	As Recorded In Other Journals			Date Recovered
	Clark	Ordway	Whitehouse	
2 Lead Canisters of Powder	X			Found and returned by Nez Perce 7 May 1806

Source: Gary E. Moulton, *The Definitive Journals of Lewis and Clark* (Lincoln: University of Nebraska Press, 2002), 4:274-77, 4:334, 4:370, 5:125, 7:220, 7:235, 8:172.

Bibliography

Books

Ambrose, Stephen E. *Undaunted Courage: Meriwether Lewis, Thomas Jefferson, and the Opening of the American West*. New York: Simon and Schuster, 1997.

Clarke, Charles G. *The Men of the Lewis and Clark Expedition: A Biographical Roster of the Fifty-One Members and a Composite Diary of Their Activities from All Known Sources*. Lincoln: University of Nebraska Press, 2002.

Chuinard, Eldon G. *Only One Man Died: The Medical Aspects of the Lewis & Clark Expedition*. Fairfield, WA: Ye Galleon Press, 1998.

Collinder, Per. *A History of Maritime Navigation*. New York: St. Martin's Press, 1955.

Coues, Elliot, ed. *The History of the Lewis and Clark Expedition*. 3 Vols. New York: Francis P. Harper, 1883; Reprint, New York: Dover Publications, 1950.

Flayderman, Norm. *Flayderman's Guide to Antique American Firearms and Their Values*. Northbrook, IL: DBI Books, 1994.

Gibson, Edmond A. *Basic Seamanship and Navigation*. New York: McGraw-Hill, 1951.

Heitman, Francis B. *Historical Register and Dictionary of the United States Army, From Its Organization, September 29, 1789, to March 2, 1903*. 2 Vols. Urbana: University of Illinois Press, 1965.

Hicks, James E. *U.S. Military Firearms 1776-1956*. La Canada, CA: James E. Hicks & Son, 1962.

Jackson, Donald, ed. *Letters of the Lewis and Clark Expedition, with Related Documents: 1783-1854*. 2 Vols. 2nd ed. Urbana: University of Illinois Press, 1978.

MacGregor, Carol L., ed. *The Journals of Patrick Gass: Member of the Lewis and Clark Expedition*. Missoula, MT: Mountain Press Publishing Company, 1997.

Moulton, Gary E., ed. *The Definitive Journals of Lewis and Clark*. 11 Vols. Lincoln: University of Nebraska Press, 2002-2003.

Peck, David J. *Or Perish in the Attempt: Wilderness Medicine in the Lewis and Clark Expedition*. Helena, MT: Farcountry Press, 2002.

Ronda, James P. *Lewis and Clark Among the Indians*. Lincoln: University of Nebraska Press, 1984.

Russell, Carl P. *Guns On The Early Frontiers: A History of Firearms From Colonial Times Through The Years of the Western Fur Trade*. Lincoln: University of Nebraska Press, 1957.

Schmidt, Milton O. *Fundamentals of Surveying*. Urbana: University of Illinois Press, 1969.

Smith, Merritt R. *Harpers Ferry Armory and the New Technology, The Challenge of Change*. Ithaca, NY: Cornell University Press. 1977.

Thwaites, Reuben Gold, ed. *Original Journals of the Lewis and Clark Expedition*. 8 Vols. New York: Dodd, Mead & Company, 1904; New York: DSI Digital Reproduction, 2001.

Periodicals

Boss, Richard C. "Keelboat, Pirogue, and Canoe: Vessels Used by the Lewis and Clark Corps of Discovery." *Nautical Research Journal* (June 1999), 68-87.

Chuinard, Eldon G. "Where Did the Lewis and Clark Expedition Start?" *We Proceeded On* 8 (May 1982), 14-17.

Cutright, Paul R. "Contributions of Philadelphia to Lewis and Clark History." *We Proceeded On*, supplementary publication no. 6 (June 2000), 1-44.

Foley, William. "The Lewis and Clark Expedition's Silent Partners: The Chouteau Brothers of St. Louis." *Missouri Historical Review,* (Spring 1983), 131-46.

Jeffrey, Joseph D. "Meriwether Lewis at Harpers Ferry." *We Proceeded On* 20 (November 1994), 14-21.

Lankiewicz, Donald P. "The Camp on the Wood River: A Winter of Preparation for the Lewis and Clark Expedition." *Journal of the Illinois State Historical Society* 75, no. 2 (1982), 115-20.

Large, Arlen J. "Additions to the Party: How the Expedition Grew and Grew." *We Proceeded On* 16 (February 1990), 4-11.

Olson, Kirk. "A Lewis and Clark Rifle?" *American Rifleman* (May 1985), 23-25, 66-68.

Ronda, James P. "Exploring the Explorers: Great Plains Peoples and the Lewis and Clark Expedition." *Great Plains Quarterly* 13, no. 2 (1993), 81-90.

_____. "'A Knowledge of Distant Parts' The Shaping of the Lewis and Clark Expedition." *Montana The Magazine of Western History* (Autumn 1991), 4-19.

Steele, Volney. "Lewis and Clark: Military Explorers, Scientists, and Physicians." *Military History of the West* 31, no. 1 (2001), 51-65.

Will, Drake W. "The Medical and Surgical Practice of the Lewis and Clark Expedition." *Journal of the History of Medicine and Allied Sciences* 14, no. 3 (1959), 273-97.

Woolworth, Alan R. "New Light on Fort Mandan: A Wintering Post of the Lewis and Clark Expedition to the Pacific." *North Dakota History* 55, no. 3 (1988), 3-14.

Other Sources

Allie, Stephen J. "The Uniforms of the Lewis and Clark Expedition." Frontier Army Museum. Fort Leavenworth, KS, 2002.

Ifland, Peter. "The History of the Sextant."Article available on-line. http://www.mat.uc. pt/~helios/Mestre/Novemb00/H61iflan.htm. Internet. Accessed 1 February 2003.

About the Author:

Major Donald L. Carr is the Chief of Logistics Readiness for Joint Interagency Task Force South located in Key West, Florida. He holds an M.M.A.S. (Military History) from the US Army Command and General Staff College and a B.A. degree in European History from the State University of New York at Albany.